Handbook
of
Forensic Services

Attention Authors

'We Convert Fighters into Writers'. That's the motto of Manas Publications since more than four decades. Our message to the world is that India can win the battle not only by the bullet but also by the pen. There is no dearth of intellectuals in our country, but their knowledge is confined to them only. No sincere effort has been made by any other publisher to channelise their knowledge in national interest. That is why the talent of a large number of intellectuals remains latent. An author transforms his knowledge into a manuscript, and it is our job to spread his/her knowledge by converting it into a beautiful book. For over four decades, Manas has been motivating the intellectuals by publishing their manuscripts and would like to publish your manuscript too. If you or your colleagues have any manuscript ready for publication or are working on it, kindly contact us with detailed synopsis and list of contents. We will transform your work into a valuable publication. If you wish, we can also suggest you the suitable subjects for writing the books related to your area of expertise. Manas is known for its publishing quality and commitments. We take utmost care in production and give wide publicity to the book as well as its author through our national and international distribution network.

Handbook
of
Forensic Services

Department of the Army, USA

Manas Publications
(We Convert Fighters into Writers)
New Delhi - 110 002 (INDIA)

MANAS PUBLICATIONS
(We Convert Fighters into Writers)
(Publishers, Library Suppliers, Importers & Exporters)
4402/5-A, Ansari Road (Opp. HDFC Bank)
Darya Ganj, New Delhi-110 002 (India)
Off. Å 23260783, 23265523, Fax: 011-23272766
E-mail: manaspublications@gmail.com
manaspublications@yahoo.com

ISBN 978-81-7049-394-5
Rs. 495/-

Typeset at
Manas Publications

Printed in India at
HS Offsets, Delhi
and published by Mrs. Suman Lata for
Manas Publications, 4402/5-A, Ansari Road
(Opp. HDFC Bank),Darya Ganj,
New Delhi-110 002 (INDIA)

Contents

Introduction

The *Handbook of Forensic Services* provides guidance and procedures for safe and efficient methods of collecting, preserving, packaging, and shipping evidence and describes the forensic examinations performed by the FBI's Laboratory Division and Operational Technology Division.

FBI Forensic Services

The successful investigation and prosecution of crimes require, in most cases, the collection, preservation, and forensic analysis of evidence. Forensic analysis of evidence is often crucial to determinations of guilt or innocence.

The FBI has one of the largest and most comprehensive forensic laboratories in the world, and the FBI Laboratory is accredited by the American Society of Crime Laboratory Directors/Laboratory Accreditation Board. The forensic services of the FBI Laboratory Division and the Operational Technology Division are available to the following:

- FBI field offices and legal attachés.
- US attorneys, military tribunals, and other federal agencies for civil and criminal matters.
- State, county, and municipal law enforcement agencies in the United States and territorial possessions for criminal matters.

All forensic services, including expert witness testimonies, are rendered free of cost; however, the following limitations apply:

- No examination will be conducted on evidence that has been previously subjected to the same type of examination. Exceptions may be granted when there are reasons for a re-examination. These reasons should be explained in separate letters from the director of the laboratory that conducted the original examination, the prosecuting attorney, and the investigating agency.
- No request for an examination will be accepted from laboratories having the capability of conducting the examination. Exceptions may be granted upon approval of the FBI Laboratory Director or a designee.
- No testimony will be furnished if testimony on the same subject and in the same case is provided for the prosecution by another expert.
- No request for an examination will be accepted from a non-federal law enforcement agency in civil matters.

In addition, when submitting evidence to the FBI Laboratory, contributors acknowledge the following:

- FBI examiners will choose appropriate technical processes to address the contributor's request for examination.
- Depending on the caseload of the Laboratory and the needs of the contributor, evidence examinations may be subcontracted.
- An FBI Laboratory Report of Examination may contain the opinions and/or interpretations of the examiner(s) who issued the report.

Violent Crime Versus Property Crime

The FBI accepts evidence related to all crimes under investigation by FBI field offices; however, it accepts from state and local law enforcement agencies only evidence related to violent crime investigations. The FBI does not routinely accept evidence from state and local law enforcement agencies in cases involving property crimes unless there was personal injury or intent to cause personal injury. These guidelines help to ensure that the FBI continues to provide timely forensic assistance to law enforcement agencies investigating crimes of violence or threatened violence. Additional restrictions may be imposed on case acceptance to achieve this goal.

At the discretion of the FBI Laboratory Director or a designee, the FBI may accept evidence from property crime cases. Such exceptions will be considered on a case-by-case basis and should not be regarded as setting a precedent for future case acceptance. All accepted cases will be afforded the full range of forensic services provided by the FBI.

The following are examples of property crimes that are not routinely accepted for examinations:

- Arson of unoccupied residential and commercial buildings and property.
- Explosive incidents and hoaxes targeting unoccupied residential and commercial buildings and property.
- Vandalism and malicious mischief directed toward residential or commercial buildings and property.
- Non-fatal traffic accidents involving speedometer and headlight examinations except in cases involving law enforcement and government officials.
- Hit-and-run automobile accidents not involving personal injury.
- Automobile theft, except automobile theft rings or carjackings.
- Breaking and entering.
- Burglary.
- Minor theft (under $100,000).
- Minor fraud (under $100,000).

Chapter 1

Submitting Evidence

Requesting Evidence Examinations

All requests for evidence examinations should be in writing, on agency letterhead, and addressed to the FBI Laboratory Evidence Control Unit, unless otherwise indicated in the **Examinations** section.

Do not submit multiple cases under a single communication. Each case should be submitted with a separate communication and packaged separately.

All international law enforcement agency/police requests should be coordinated through the appropriate FBI legal attaché (LEGAT). LEGATs should fax the request to the Evidence Control Unit, 703-632-8334, prior to submitting any evidence to the Laboratory. Questions concerning international submissions should be directed to 703-632-8360.

Requests for evidence examinations must contain the following information:

- The submitting contact person's name, agency, address, and telephone number.

- Previous case-identification numbers, evidence submissions, and communications relating to the case.
- Description of the nature and the basic facts of the case as they pertain to evidence examinations.
- The name(s) of and descriptive data about the individual(s) involved (subject, suspect, victim, or a combination of those categories) and the agency-assigned case-identification number.
- The name of the prosecutor assigned, if available.
- A list of the evidence being submitted "herewith" (enclosed) or "under separate cover".
    - *Herewith* is limited to small items of evidence that are not endangered by transmitting in an envelope. Write on the envelope before placing evidence inside to avoid damaging or altering the evidence. The written communication should state: "**Submitted herewith are the following items of evidence**".
    - Separate cover is used to ship numerous or bulky items of evidence. Include a copy of the communication requesting the examinations. The written communication should state: "Submitted under separate cover by [list the method of shipment] are the following items of evidence".
- What type(s) of examination(s) is/are requested.
- Where the evidence should be returned and where the Laboratory report should be sent. A street address must be included.
- A statement if the evidence was previously examined, if there is local controversy, or if other law enforcement agencies have an interest in the case.

Packaging and Shipping Evidence

- Prior to packaging and shipping evidence, call the pertinent unit for specific instructions.
- Take precautions to preserve the evidence.
- Wrap and seal each item of evidence separately to avoid contamination.
- Place the evidence in a clean, dry, and previously unused inner container.
- Seal the inner container with tamper-evident or filament tape.
- Affix EVIDENCE and BIOHAZARD labels, if appropriate, on the inner container. If any of the evidence needs to be examined for latent prints, affix a LATENT label on the inner container.
- Affix the evidence examination request and all case information between the inner and outer containers.
- Place the sealed inner container in a clean, dry, and previously unused outer container with clean packing materials. Do not use loose Styrofoam.
- Completely seal the outer container so that tampering with the container would be evident.
- All **shipments of suspected or confirmed hazardous materials** must comply with US Department of Transportation and International Air Transport Association regulations. Title 49 of the Code of Federal Regulations (CFR) lists specific requirements that must be observed when preparing hazardous materials for shipment by air, land, or sea. In addition, the International Air Transport Association annually publishes *Dangerous Goods Regulations* detailing how to prepare and package shipments for air transportation.

- Title 49 CFR 172.101 provides a Hazardous Materials Table that identifies items considered hazardous for the purpose of transportation. Title 49 CFR 172.101 also addresses special provisions for certain materials, hazardous materials communications, emergency response information, and training requirements for shippers. A trained and qualified evidence technician must assist with the typing, labeling, packaging, and shipping of all hazardous materials.

US Department of Transportation regulations and the following guidelines must be followed when shipping live ammunition:

  - Package and ship ammunition separately from firearm(s).
  - The outside of the container must be labeled "ORM-D, CARTRIDGES, SMALL ARMS".
  - The Declaration of Dangerous Goods must include the number of packages and the gross weight in grams of the completed packages.

- Unless otherwise indicated in the **Examinations** section, address the outer container as follows:

Evidence Control Unit, Laboratory Division, Federal Bureau of Investigation, 2501 Investigation Parkway, Quantico VA 22135

- Ship evidence by US Postal Service Registered Mail, UPS, or FedEx. Record the method of shipment and the tracking number(s) on the chain-of-custody form.

Chapter 2

Evidence Examinations

Abrasives Examinations

Examinations may determine the type of abrasive material used to sabotage engines or machinery.

Questions concerning abrasives evidence should be directed to 703-632-8441. Follow the evidence submission directions, including **Requesting Evidence Examinations** and **Packaging and Shipping Evidence**.

- Employ personnel familiar with the operations and mechanics of engines and machinery to recover abrasives.
- Abrasives settle in oil and fuel. Submit the oil and fuel from the engine pump and/or filters.
- Abrasives embed in bearings and other parts. Submit the bearings and other parts.
- Submit abrasives in heat-sealed or resealable plastic bags or paint cans. Do not use paper or glass containers.

Adhesive, Caulk, and Sealant Examinations

Adhesives, caulks, and sealants can be compared by color and chemical composition with suspected sources. The source and manufacturer of adhesives, caulks, and sealants cannot be determined by compositional analysis.

Questions concerning adhesive, caulk, and sealant evidence should be directed to 703-632-8441. Follow the evidence submission directions, including **Requesting Evidence Examinations** and **Packaging and Shipping Evidence**.

- When possible, submit the item to which the adhesive, caulk, or sealant is adhered. If this is not possible, remove a sample of the material with a clean, sharp instrument and transfer it to a resealable plastic bag or leakproof container such as a film canister or plastic pill bottle.
- Submit a suspected source. Package separately.

Anthropological Examinations

Anthropological examinations can determine whether something is a bone and, if so, whether it is human or animal in origin. Race, sex, approximate height and stature, and approximate age at death often can be determined from human remains. Damage to bone such as cuts, blunt-force trauma, and bullet holes also may be examined. Personal identifications can be made by comparing X-rays of a known individual with skeletal remains.

Anthropological examinations usually are conducted on bones sent to the Laboratory for DNA analysis or facial reproductions.

Questions concerning anthropological evidence should be directed to 703-632-8449. Follow the evidence submission directions, including **Requesting Evidence Examinations** and **Packaging and Shipping Evidence**.

- Clean and air-dry bones, if possible. Pack in paper bags and wrap in protective material such as Bubble Wrap or paper. If tissue is present on the skeletal material, refrigerate until mailing, and then ship in a Styrofoam cooler.
- Collect insect samples found on the remains in leakproof containers such as film canisters or plastic pill bottles. Call the Laboratory at **703-632-8449** for additional instructions.

Submit medical records and X-rays, if possible.

Arson Examinations

Arson examinations can determine the presence of ignitable liquids introduced to a fire scene. Examinations of debris recovered from scenes can identify gasoline, fuel oils, and speciality solvents. Examinations generally cannot identify specific brands.

Search at questioned arson scenes for the following items: candles, cigarettes, matchbooks, Molotov cocktails, fused chemical masses, or any electronic or mechanical devices an arsonist may have used. Also search for burn trails on cloth or paper, burn trails on carpeted or hardwood floors, and the removal of personal property or commercial inventory.

Questions concerning arson evidence should be directed to 703-632-7641. Follow the evidence submission directions, including **Requesting Evidence Examinations** and **Packaging and Shipping Evidence**.

Ignitable liquids are volatile and easily lost through evaporation. Preserve evidence in airtight containers such as metal cans, glass jars, or heat-sealed plastic bags approved for fire debris. Do not fill the containers to the top. Pack to prevent breakage.

Audio Examinations

Audio examinations are conducted by the FBI's Operational Technology Division (OTD), Digital Evidence Laboratory (DEL), Forensic Audio, Video, and Image Analysis Unit (FAVIAU). The OTD DEL has different acceptance criteria and a different physical address than the FBI Laboratory, as described below.

Authenticity

Authenticity examinations are conducted to determine whether audio recordings are original, continuous, unaltered, and consistent with the operation of the recording device used to make the recording.

Enhancement

Enhancement examinations are conducted to selectively reduce interfering noise on audio recordings to improve the intelligibility.

Voice Comparisons

Spectrographic examinations compare an unknown recorded voice sample with a known verbatim voice exemplar produced on a similar transmission-and-recording device such as the telephone. Decisions regarding spectrographic voice comparisons are not conclusive. The results of voice comparisons are provided for investigative guidance only.

Signal Analysis

Signal analysis examinations are conducted to identify, compare, and interpret such signals as gunshots and telephone touch tones.

Damaged Media

Audio recordings can be repaired, restored, or retrieved for playback and examination, if damage is not too extensive.

Questions concerning audio examinations should be directed to 703-985-1393. Questions concerning audio evidence should be directed to 703-985-1388.

Audio examinations may not be submitted directly from entities outside the FBI. State, local, or international agency cases must be submitted by the FBI field office servicing the area and must meet one of the following two criteria: 1) the state, local, or international case has a nexus to an ongoing FBI investigation or 2) the FBI division head deems that the case is of enough regional importance to merit the dedication of federal resources to the state, local, or international case. These criteria shall be met with a written statement from the division head (Special Agent in Charge). FBI entities may submit cases directly.

Follow the evidence submission directions, including **Requesting Evidence Examinations** and **Packaging and Shipping Evidence**.

- Write-protect the original recording, which may include finalizing CD and DVD media.
- Submit original audio recordings.
- Identify known and questioned voice samples.
- Label the outer container "FRAGILE, SENSITIVE ELECTRONIC EQUIPMENT" or "FRAGILE, SENSITIVE AUDIO/VIDEO MEDIA" and "KEEP AWAY FROM MAGNETS OR MAGNETIC FIELDS".
- Address the outer container as follows:

Forensic Program, Building - 27958A, Engineering Research Facility, Federal Bureau of Investigation, Quantico - VA 22135

Bank Security Dye Examinations

Bank dye packs contain dye to stain money and clothing and tear gas to disorient a robber. Items such as money and clothing can be analyzed for the presence of bank security dye and tear gas.

Questions concerning bank security dye evidence should be directed to 703-632-8441. Follow the evidence submission directions, including **Requesting Evidence Examinations** and **Packaging and Shipping Evidence**.

- Only evidence with visible red or pink stains will be examined.
- Do not submit large-stained evidence (e.g., car seats). When possible, cut a small sample of the stained area and submit in a heat-sealed or resealable plastic bag. Collect an unstained control sample, package separately, and submit it with the dye-stained evidence. When cutting is not possible, transfer questioned stains by rubbing with a clean (dry or wet with alcohol) cotton swab. Use an unstained swab as a control. Air-dry the swab and pack in a heat-sealed or resealable plastic bag.

Building Materials Examinations

Examinations can compare building materials such as brick, mortar, plaster, stucco, cement, and concrete.

Questions concerning building materials evidence should be directed to 703-632-8449. Follow the evidence submission directions, including **Requesting Evidence Examinations** and **Packaging and Shipping Evidence**.

- When building materials are penetrated or damaged, debris can adhere to people, clothing, tools, bags, and stolen items and can transfer to vehicles. If possible, submit the evidence to the Laboratory for examiners to remove the debris. Package each item of evidence in a separate paper bag. Do not process tools for latent prints.

- Collect known samples from the penetrated or damaged areas.
- Ship known and questioned debris separately to avoid contamination. Submit known and questioned debris in leakproof containers such as film canisters or plastic pill bottles. Do not use paper or glass containers. Pack to keep lumps intact.

Bullet Jacket Alloy Examinations

Elemental analysis of bullet jackets can be done when a bullet has fragmented so that individual pieces cannot be used for comparison with test-fired ammunition from a firearm or in the absence of a firearm or the lead component of the bullet. This analysis may be helpful when there are multiple shooters and types of jacketed ammunition. Alloy classification can differentiate among bullet jacket alloys of different manufacturers or among the bullet jacket alloys in manufacturers' production lines.

Questions concerning bullet jacket alloy examinations should be directed to 703-632-8441. Follow the evidence submission directions, including **Requesting Evidence Examinations** and **Packaging and Shipping Evidence.**

- Ammunition components such as bullets, cartridge cases, and shotshell casings can be sent via Registered Mail through the US Postal Service. Evidence must be packaged separately with the date, time, location, collector's name, case number, and evidence number written on the container.
- US Department of Transportation regulations and the following guidelines must be followed when shipping live ammunition:

- Package and ship ammunition separately from firearm(s).
- The outside of the container must be labeled "ORM-D, CARTRIDGES, SMALL ARMS".
- The Declaration of Dangerous Goods must include the number of package(s) and the gross weight in grams of the completed package(s).

◦ Do not mark bullets, cartridges, cartridge cases, shotshells, or shotshell casings. The date, time, location, collector's name, case number, and evidence number must be on the container.

Chemical Examinations of General Unknowns

General unknowns include powders, liquids, and stains that are of indeterminate origin or cannot be readily classified. Full identification of an unknown may not always be possible; however, general classification of a substance is usually achievable.

When comparison samples are available, it may be possible to comment regarding the consistency of the unknown substance compared with a known sample.

Call the Laboratory at 703-632-8441 prior to submitting general unknowns to ensure that the evidence will be accepted for examination. The communication accompanying the evidence must reference the telephone conversation accepting the evidence.

Questions concerning examinations of general unknowns should be directed to 703-632-8441. Follow the evidence submission directions, including **Requesting Evidence Examinations** and **Packaging and Shipping Evidence**.

- Submit powder and liquid samples in leak-proof containers.

Do not submit large-stained evidence. When possible, cut a small sample of the stained area and submit in a heat-sealed or resealable plastic bag. Collect an unstained control sample, package separately, and submit it with the stained evidence. When cutting is not possible, transfer questioned stains by rubbing with a clean (dry or wet with alcohol) cotton swab. Use an unstained swab as a control. Air-dry the swab and pack in a heat-sealed or resealable plastic bag.

Computer Examinations

Content

Examinations can determine what type of data files are on a computer.

Comparison

Examinations can compare data files with known documents and data files.

Transaction

Examinations can determine the time and sequence that data files were created.

Extraction

Data files can be extracted from the computer or computer storage media.

Deleted Data Files

Deleted data files can be recovered from the computer or computer storage media.

Format Conversion

Data files can be converted from one format to another.

Keyword Searching

Data files can be searched for a word or phrase and all occurrences recorded.

Passwords

Passwords can be recovered and used to decrypt encoded files.

Limited Source Code

Source code can be analyzed and compared.

Call the Computer Analysis Response Team at 703-985-1302 to request a search or field examination. Submit requests at least one week in advance.

Obtain as much of the following information as possible prior to submitting a request:

- Determine the type(s) of computers and operating systems.
- If applicable, determine the type of network software, the location of the network servers, and the number of computers on the network.
- Determine whether encryption and/or password protection is used.
- Specify whether a seizure of computers and media or an on-site examination is required.

Questions concerning computer evidence should be directed to 703-985-1302. Follow the evidence submission directions, including **Requesting Evidence Examinations** and **Packaging and Shipping Evidence**.

- For most examinations, submit only the central processing units and the internal and external storage media.

- Use a sturdy cardboard container when shipping computer components. If possible, use the original packing case with the fitted padding. Use large plastic Bubble Wrap or foam rubber pads as packing. Do not use loose Styrofoam because it lodges inside computers and components and creates static charges that can cause data loss or damage to circuit boards. Seal the container with a strong packing tape.
- Pack and ship central processing units in the upright position. Label the outside container "THIS END UP".
- Disks, cartridges, tapes, and hard drives must be packed to avoid movement during shipping.
- Label the outer container "FRAGILE, SENSITIVE ELECTRONIC EQUIPMENT" and "KEEP AWAY FROM MAGNETS OR MAGNETIC FIELDS".
- Address the outer container as follows:

Forensic Program, Building - 27958A, Engineering Research Facility, Federal Bureau of Investigation, Quantico - VA 22135

Controlled Substance Examinations

Controlled substance examinations can establish trace-drug presence, identity, and quantity.

Bulk Drugs

The Laboratory limits the quantity of bulk drugs that it will analyze. Quantities exceeding 100 grams of suspected marijuana or 10 grams of all other suspected drugs including cocaine, methamphetamine, and heroin will be returned unanalyzed. The Laboratory usually analyzes only drugs seized in federal investigations.

Drug Residue

Requests for drug residue examinations on evidence will be accepted only when the evidence is properly packaged to avoid contamination. Drug residue examinations of currency are performed only on a limited basis.

Call the Laboratory at 703-632-8441 prior to submitting drugs or currency to ensure that the evidence will be accepted for examination. The communication accompanying the evidence must reference the telephone conversation accepting the evidence.

Questions concerning controlled substance evidence should be directed to 703-632-8441. Follow the evidence submission directions, including **Requesting Evidence Examinations** and **Packaging and Shipping Evidence**.

- Submit evidence in separate heat-sealed or resealable plastic bags.
- Fold clothing to preserve trace evidence.
- Do not submit used drug field-test kits with evidence.

Crime Scene Surveys, Documentation, and Reconstruction

Visual information specialists receive data from the field or travel to the field to collect it. They then use the data to prepare two- and three-dimensional digital or physical crime scene reconstructions as well as computer animations or models that depict bullet trajectory, line-of-sight analysis, and vehicular-, human-, or object-movement analysis.

Questions concerning crime scene surveys, documentation, and reconstruction should be directed to 703-632-8194.

Cryptanalysis and Racketeering Record Examinations

Cryptanalysis

Cryptanalysis examinations involve the analysis of encoded and enciphered documents used by terrorists, foreign intelligence agents, violent criminals, street and prison gangs, and organized crime groups. Encrypted documents may be faxed or e-mailed for immediate decryption. Call **703-632-7356** or **703-632-7334** for contact information.

Drug Records

Drug records are examined to determine the overall scope of the businesses, including the hierarchy, type of drugs distributed, gross sales, gross or net weights or quantities, price structures, and other pertinent information.

Gambling

Gambling examinations include the interpretation of records from sports and horse bookmaking businesses, Internet gambling operations, numbers or lottery operations, and other gambling businesses.

Loan-sharking

Loan-sharking records are examined to determine the amounts of the loans, amounts paid in interest and principal, number of loans, and interest rates.

Money-Laundering

Money-laundering records are examined to determine the scope of the operations, the amounts laundered, how the funds were laundered, and any other illegal activities.

Prostitution

Prostitution records are examined to determine the scope of the businesses, including the number of employees and their roles, gross and net revenues, and other financial and organizational information.

Questions concerning cryptanalysis and racketeering record evidence should be directed to 703-632-7356 or 703-632-7334. Follow the evidence submission directions, including **Requesting Evidence Examinations** and **Packaging and Shipping Evidence**.

Demonstrative Evidence

Visual information specialists prepare a wide array of demonstrative evidence for investigative and prosecutorial purposes. These items include charts, maps, diagrams, illustrations, and animated and digitally interactive presentations.

Questions concerning demonstrative evidence should be directed to 703-632-8194.

DNA Examinations

Deoxyribonucleic acid (DNA) is analyzed in body-fluid stains and other biological tissues recovered from items of evidence. The results of DNA testing on evidence samples are compared with the results of DNA analysis of reference samples collected from known individuals. Such analyses can associate victims and suspects with each other, with evidence items, or with a crime scene.

There are two types of DNA used in forensic analyses. Nuclear DNA (nDNA) is the more discriminating of the two types and is typically analyzed in evidence containing blood, semen, saliva, body tissue, and hairs that have tissue at their root ends. The power of nDNA testing done by the DNA Analysis Unit I (DNAUI) lies in its ability to potentially identify an individual as being the source of the DNA obtained from an evidence item to a reasonable degree of scientific certainty, as well as the definitive power of exclusion. Additionally, where appropriate, the DNA-typing results from evidence items (including items related to missing persons) examined in the DNAUI may be uploaded into the Combined DNA Index System (CODIS) database.

Mitochondrial DNA (mtDNA) is typically analyzed in evidence containing naturally shed hairs, hair fragments, bones, and teeth. Typically, these items contain low concentrations of degraded DNA, making them unsuitable for nDNA examinations. The high sensitivity of mtDNA analysis allows scientists to obtain information from old items of evidence associated with cold cases, samples from mass disasters, and small pieces of evidence containing little biological material. Additionally, the maternal inheritance of mtDNA allows scientists to compare a mtDNA profile to reference samples from that person's mother, brother(s), sister(s), or any other maternally related individuals. All of these individuals have the same mtDNA profiles because all maternal relatives inherit their mtDNA from their mother. Because multiple individuals can have the same mtDNA type, unique identifications are not possible using mtDNA analysis. However, mtDNA performed by the DNA Analysis Unit II is an excellent technique to use for obtaining information when nDNA analysis is not feasible. Additionally, the mtDNA-typing results related to missing-person cases may be uploaded into the CODIS database. **Questions concerning nuclear DNA testing should be directed to 703-632-8446. Questions concerning mitochondrial DNA testing should be directed to 703-632-7572.** Follow the evidence submission directions, including **Requesting Evidence Examinations** and **Packaging and Shipping Evidence.**

Case Acceptance Policy of the DNA Analysis Unit I

- The DNAUI accepts FBI cases for serological and nDNA analysis. FBI cases are prioritized according to the FBI's priorities of counter-terrorism; cyber-based/high-technology crimes; public corruption; civil rights; transnational/national criminal organizations/enterprises; major white-collar crime; significant violent crime; and support of local, state, federal, and international agencies. This includes examinations that characterize biological stains and may identify the source of a stain on an evidentiary item.
- Cases are accepted provided that:
  1. The submitting agency is not served by another government forensic DNA laboratory.
  2. The submitted case has not been examined previously by another laboratory.

Case Consideration Policy

- The DNAUI supports the National Missing Person DNA Database (NMPDD) Program. Cases must be submitted through an NMPDD Program Manager for entry into the Biological Relatives of Missing Persons or Unidentified Human Remains Indexes. The NMPDD provides investigators with an opportunity to identify missing and unidentified persons on a national level.
- The DNAUI maintains the Federal Convicted Offender (FCO) Program, which supports the collection and nDNA analysis of samples collected from more than 500 sites across the United States.

- The DNAUI requires known reference sample(s) for comparison with evidence materials. DNA profiles located in the National DNA Index System (NDIS) Convicted Offender database cannot be used as references.
- The DNAUI does not conduct low-copy-number (LCN) or "touch DNA" examinations (i.e., DNA from fingerprints, pieces of paper, handled objects, etc.). Items such as steering wheels and firearms may be appropriate for analysis.
- The DNAUI does not perform kinship analysis. Questions concerning kinship, paternity/maternity comparisons, etc, should be directed to the DNAUI at **703-632-8446**.

As necessary:

- DNAUI cases may be prioritized according to scheduled trial dates or other case-specific information.
- The DNAUI does not examine evidence from property crime cases unless violence that results in bodily harm is used in the commission of the crime.
- For cases in which the FBI Laboratory has conducted previous DNA or serological testing, a review of the case file will be conducted to determine if additional examinations will be conducted.

Case Acceptance Policy of the DNA Analysis Unit II

All FBI cases that meet the suitability guidelines (outlined below) will be considered for mtDNA analysis in the DNAUII. Cases involving terrorism are given highest priority, followed by counter-intelligence matters and violent crimes. Questions regarding case and evidence suitability should be directed to the DNAUII at **703-632-7572**.

State and local law enforcement agencies needing mtDNA analysis must contact the DNAUII for more information regarding evidence submission. Agencies may call **703-632-7572** to discuss the needs of the investigation and the evidence, following the suitability guidelines outlined below. Analysis of the evidence will be performed by one of the unit's regional mtDNA laboratories and is cost-free to state and local law enforcement agencies in the United States and its territories. Travel expenses for examiners testifying in state and local cases are also paid by the FBI Laboratory. FBI cntities may refer to the FBI Laboratory/DNAUII web page on the FBI intranet for additional information on the regional mtDNA laboratories.

Missing-person cases involving unidentified human remains and relatives of missing persons arc managed and entered into the NDIS in the DNAUII by members of the NMPDD Program. Evidence from these investigations also undergoes mtDNA analysis in the DNAUII or in one of the regional mtDNA laboratories. Contact the NMPDD Program Manager at **703-632-7582** for questions regarding missing-person evidence submission. FBI entities may refer to the FBI Laboratory/DNAUII web page on the FBI intranet for additional information on the NMPDD Program.

Suitability of Mitochondrial DNA Analysis

Mitochondrial DNA analysis has been applied successfully to evidence from violent crimes, typically homicide, sexual assault, and assault. It is important to remember, however, that mtDNA analysis is appropriate in only a small portion of cases where mtDNA evidence is present.

Experience shows that about 75 percent of cases in which mtDNA analysis is actually performed involve hair evidence where only the hair shaft is present. Most often, mtDNA analysis is justified for hair evidence when no tissue is present on the hair root. Mitochondrial DNA analysis in missing-person cases is appropriate only when bone or teeth specimens can be verified as of human origin.

To avoid the misapplication of mtDNA analysis resources, cases must be reviewed carefully for their scenarios, the possibility of other tests on available evidence (e.g., nDNA), and the selection of specimens having the greatest probative value.

Regardless of the type of biological evidence, mtDNA analysis *generally will not be performed* when nDNA results exist on items of similar origin. For example, if nDNA results are obtained from semen identified on a victim's vaginal swabs and there is no allegation of multiple assailants, mtDNA analysis would not be performed on an associated pubic hair found in the pubic-hair combings of the victim.

Current forensic mtDNA techniques cannot effectively distinguish between sources or relative quantities of DNA. Consequently, mtDNA is not appropriate for evidence containing possible mixed sources of DNA *such as semen stains from sexual assaults.*

Mitochondrial DNA analysis *generally will not be performed on bloodstains* unless the victim's reference samples are not available or other appropriate reference samples are unavailable for nDNA analysis. For example, a kidnapping victim is missing, but a bloodstain is found in the suspect's vehicle and only a maternal relative's (e.g., mother, sibling) reference sample is available for the victim. In that case, mtDNA analysis could be conducted using a portion of the vehicle bloodstain, the maternal relative's reference sample, and the suspect's known sample.

Mitochondrial DNA Analysis of Hair Evidence

Mitochondrial DNA analysis should be performed on probative hair samples *only if they are deemed* ***unsuitable*** *for nDNA analysis*. Only those hairs having greatest probative value should be subjected to mtDNA analysis. If several similar probative hair specimens are submitted from one source of evidence, mtDNA analysis should be performed on only 1–2 hairs. For example, if ten hairs collected from a victim's body are microscopically associated with the suspect, no more than two hairs will bc analyzed.

Submission guidelines for mtDNA cases must include the following points for hair evidence:

- Known victim hair samples (of all types) must be submitted to determine whether evidence hairs are similar or dissimilar to the victim's hair.
- If evidence includes specimens dissimilar to the victim, known suspect hair samples (of all types) should be obtained.

Mitochondrial DNA analysis generally will be performed on all probative microscopic hair associations. In addition, the following types of hairs are considered for mtDNA analysis, if probative:

- Hairs that exhibit "microscopic similarities and slight differences" (e.g., because of prolonged time between the crime and collection of reference samples, environmental or artificial changes to hair, or the suitability of reference samples or questioned hair).
- Hairs that are not suitable for microscopic comparison purposes (e.g., body-area hairs, hair fragments, or any other factor that eliminates the possibility of

performing a comparison). In such cases, however, the hair must be probative (e.g., apparent foreign hair in the pubic-hair combing of the victim).

- Hairs that are suitable for microscopic comparison purposes but, for valid reasons, are not suitable to compare with the pertinent reference sample (e.g., hair deposited 10 years prior to the collection of the reference hair sample, reference sample is from an individual whose hair is artificially treated after the crime date). Regardless, the hair must be probative.

Unidentified Human Remains

Prior to mtDNA analysis, bone or teeth specimens should be examined by a forensic anthropologist or odontologist or a similarly qualified individual. Submissions of such items should be accompanied by a written report that verifies human origin by a qualified expert.

Documenting, Collecting, Packaging, and Preserving DNA Evidence

If DNA evidence is not properly documented, collected, packaged, and preserved, it will not meet the legal and scientific requirements for admissibility in a court of law.

- If DNA evidence is not properly documented, its origin can be questioned.
- If it is not properly collected, biological activity can be lost.
- If it is not properly packaged, contamination can occur.
- If it is not properly preserved, decomposition and deterioration can occur.

When DNA evidence is transferred by direct or secondary (indirect) means, it remains on surfaces by absorption or adherence. In general, liquid biological evidence is absorbed into surfaces, and solid biological evidence adheres to surfaces. Collecting, packaging, and preserving DNA evidence depends on the liquid or solid state and the condition of the evidence.

The more evidence retains its original integrity until it reaches the Laboratory, the greater the possibility of conducting useful examinations. It may be necessary to use a variety of techniques to collect suspected body-fluid evidence.

Collecting Known Samples

Blood

- Only qualified medical personnel should collect blood samples from a person.
- Collect at least two 5-ml tubes of blood in purple-top tubes, which contain EDTA as a preservative, for DNA analysis. Collect drug or alcohol-testing samples in gray-top tubes, which contain NaF (sodium fluoride).
- Label each tube with the date, time, person's name, location, collector's name, case number, and evidence number.
- Refrigerate, do not freeze, liquid blood samples (tubes may break if frozen). Use cold packs, not dry ice, during shipping.
- Pack liquid blood tubes individually in Styrofoam or cylindrical tubes with absorbent material surrounding the tubes.
- Package blood samples from different individuals separately.

- Label the outer container "KEEP IN A COOL, DRY PLACE", "REFRIGERATE ON ARRIVAL", and "BIOHAZARD".
- Submit to the Laboratory as soon as possible.

Buccal (Oral) Swabs

- Use clean cotton swabs to collect buccal (oral) samples. Rub the inside surfaces of the cheeks thoroughly.
- Air-dry the swabs and place in clean paper or an envelope with sealed corners. Do not use plastic containers.
- Identify each sample with the date, time, person's name, location, collector's name, case number, and evidence number.
- Package oral samples from different individuals separately.
- Buccal samples do not need to be refrigerated.
- Submit to the Laboratory as soon as possible.
- If a reference blood or oral sample cannot be obtained, an alternate reference sample may be submitted (for nuclear examinations only). This may include such items as surgical samples, Pap smear slides, pulled teeth, or a toothbrush or item of clothing known to be used solely by the individual of interest.

Blood on a Person

- Absorb suspected liquid blood onto a clean cotton cloth or swab. Air-dry the cloth or swab and pack in clean paper or an envelope with sealed corners. Do not use plastic containers.
- Absorb suspected dried blood onto a clean cotton cloth or swab moistened with distilled water.

Air-dry the cloth or swab and pack in clean paper or an envelope with sealed corners. Do not use plastic containers.

Blood on Surfaces or in Snow or Water

- Absorb suspected liquid blood or blood clots onto a clean cotton cloth or swab. Air-dry the cloth or swab and pack in clean paper or an envelope with sealed corners. Do not use plastic containers.
- Collect suspected blood in snow or water immediately to avoid further dilution. Eliminate as much snow as possible. Place in a clean, airtight container. Freeze the evidence and submit to the Laboratory as soon as possible.

Bloodstains

- Air-dry suspected wet bloodstained garments. Wrap dried bloodstained garments in clean paper. Do not place wet or dried garments in plastic or airtight containers. Place all debris or residue from the garments in clean paper or an envelope with sealed corners.
- Air-dry small suspected wet bloodstained objects and submit the objects to the Laboratory. Preserve bloodstain patterns. Avoid creating additional stain patterns during drying and packaging. Pack to prevent stain removal by abrasive action during shipping. Pack in clean paper. Do not use plastic containers.
- When possible, cut a large sample of suspected bloodstains from immovable objects with a clean, sharp instrument. Pack to prevent stain removal by abrasive action during shipping. Pack in clean paper. Do not use plastic containers.

- Absorb suspected dried bloodstains on immovable objects onto a clean cotton cloth or swab moistened with distilled water. Air-dry the cloth or swab and pack in clean paper or an envelope with sealed corners. Do not use plastic containers.

Blood Examination Request Letter

A blood examination request letter must contain the following information:

- A brief statement of facts relating to the case.
- Claims made by the suspect(s) regarding the source of the blood.
- Whether animal blood is present.
- Whether the stains were laundered or diluted with other body fluids.
- Information regarding the health of the victim(s) and suspect(s), including the presence of such infections as AIDS, hepatitis, and tuberculosis.

Semen and Semen Stains

- Absorb suspected liquid semen onto a clean cotton cloth or swab. Air-dry the cloth or swab and pack in clean paper or an envelope with sealed corners. Do not use plastic containers.
- Submit small suspected dry semen-stained objects to the Laboratory. Pack to prevent stain removal by abrasive action during shipping. Pack in clean paper. Do not use plastic containers.
- When possible, cut a large sample of suspected semen stains from immovable objects with a clean, sharp instrument. Pack to prevent stain removal by abrasive action during shipping. Pack in clean paper. Do not use plastic containers.

- Absorb suspected dried semen stains on immovable objects onto a clean cotton cloth or swab moistened with distilled water. Air-dry the swab or cloth and place in clean paper or an envelope with sealed corners. Do not use plastic containers.
- Note: It is not necessary to collect reference seminal fluid for comparison. Refer to the ***Collecting Known Samples*** section for more information.

Seminal Evidence from Sexual Assault Victims

- Sexual assault victims must be medically examined in a hospital or a physician's office using a standard sexual assault evidence kit to collect vaginal, oral, and anal evidence.
- Refrigerate and submit the evidence to the Laboratory as soon as possible.

Saliva and Urine, Other Sources of Body-fluid Evidence

- Absorb suspected liquid saliva or urine onto a clean cotton cloth or swab. Air-dry the cloth or swab and pack in clean paper or an envelope with sealed corners. Do not use plastic containers.
- Submit small suspected dry saliva- or urine-stained objects to the Laboratory. Pack to prevent stain removal by abrasive action during shipping. Pack in clean paper or an envelope with sealed corners. Do not use plastic containers.
- When possible, cut a large sample of suspected saliva or urine stains from immovable objects with a clean, sharp instrument. Pack to prevent stain removal by abrasive action during shipping. Pack in clean paper. Do not use plastic containers.

- Pick up cigarette butts with gloved hands or clean forceps. Do not submit ashes. Air-dry and place the cigarette butts from the same location (e.g., ashtray) in clean paper or an envelope with sealed corners. Do not submit the ashtray unless a latent print examination is requested. Package the ashtray separately. Do not use plastic containers.
- Pick up chewing gum with gloved hands or clean forceps. Air-dry and place in clean paper or an envelope with sealed corners. Do not use plastic containers.
- Pick up envelopes and stamps with gloved hands or clean forceps and place in a clean envelope. Do not use plastic containers.

Hair

- Pick up hair carefully with clean forceps to prevent damaging the root tissue.
- Air-dry hair mixed with suspected body fluids.
- Package each group of hair separately in clean paper or an envelope with sealed corners. Do not use plastic containers.
- Refrigerate and submit to the Laboratory as soon as possible.

Tissue, Bones, and Teeth

Call the Laboratory at **703-632-7572** prior to submitting suspected tissue, bones, or teeth to ensure that the evidence will be accepted for examination. The communication accompanying the evidence must reference the telephone conversation accepting the evidence.

- Pick up suspected tissue, bones, and teeth with gloved hands or clean forceps.

- Collect 1–2 cubic inches of red skeletal muscle.
- Submit whole bones. Cutting bones increases the possibility of contamination.
- Collect teeth in the following order:
  1. Non-restored molar.
  2. Non-restored premolar.
  3. Non-restored canine.
  4. Non-restored front tooth.
  5. Restored molar.
  6. Restored premolar.
  7. Restored canine.
  8. Restored front tooth.
- Place tissue samples in a clean, airtight plastic container without formalin or formaldehyde. Place teeth and bone samples in clean paper or an envelope with sealed corners.
- Freeze the evidence, place in Styrofoam containers, and ship overnight on dry ice.

Preserving DNA Evidence–Long-Term Storage

- Blood/saliva (reference samples).
  - Refrigerate, do not freeze, liquid blood samples.
  - Store refrigerated, frozen (if dried), or at room temperature, away from light and humidity.
- Blood/semen (evidence samples).
  - Store refrigerated, frozen, or at room temperature, away from light and humidity.

- **DNA tubes/tissue samples, etc.**
  - Store refrigerated or frozen, if possible.
  - It is recommended that these samples be stored in a refrigerator/freezer and isolated from evidence that has not been examined.

Electronic Device Examinations

Commercial Electronic Devices

Examinations of commercial electronic devices—including personal digital assistants (PDAs), cellular telephones, pagers, and global positioning systems (GPSs)—can extract user- or owner-entered data and other information. In some cases, it is necessary to disassemble the devices during examination.

Interception-of-Communication Devices

Interception-of-Communication (IOC) devices are used to unlawfully intercept oral or wire communications. The devices consist of radio-frequency transmitters and receivers. Examinations are conducted to identify operating characteristics (frequency of operation, range of operation). In some cases, it is necessary to disassemble the devices during examination.

Other Electronic Devices and Circuits

Examinations on other electronic devices and circuitry—including facsimile machines, stun guns, and bomb detonators—can extract user- or owner-entered data, stored data, and other information. The examinations can identify operating characteristics and modifications made to the devices. In some cases, it is necessary to disassemble the devices and/or circuits during examination.

Questions concerning electronic device examinations should be directed to 703-985-2400. Questions concerning shipping electronic device evidence should be directed to 703-985-1388. FBI entities may refer to the Operational Technology Division/Digital Evidence Section web page on the FBI intranet for additional information regarding evidence submission.

Follow the evidence submission directions, including Requesting Evidence Examinations and Packaging and Shipping Evidence.

- Label the outer container "FRAGILE, SENSITIVE ELECTRONIC EQUIPMENT" and "KEEP AWAY FROM MAGNETS OR MAGNETIC FIELDS".
- Address the outer container as follows:

Forensic Program, Building - 27958A, Engineering Research Facility, Federal Bureau of Investigation, Quantico - VA 22135

Explosives Examinations

Evidence resulting from an apparent explosion and/or recovery of an explosive device can be examined. Examinations are based on the premise that components and accessories used to construct the devices survive the explosion, although disfigured. The examinations can accomplish the following:

- Identify the components used to construct the device, such as switches, batteries, detonators, tapes, wires, and fusing systems.
- Identify the explosive main charge.
- Determine the construction characteristics.
- Determine the manner in which the device functioned or was designed or intended to function.
- Determine the specific assembly techniques employed by the builder(s) of the device.

- Preserve the trace evidence potentially present in the devices so that it is not destroyed or damaged during the examinations.

Call the Laboratory at 703-632-7626 each time an explosive device or a related explosive item needs to be shipped. The communication accompanying the evidence must reference the telephone conversation accepting the evidence.

Questions concerning explosives evidence should be directed to 703-632-7626.

Explosives are hazardous materials and must be handled only by qualified public safety personnel, military explosives ordnance disposal personnel, or certified bomb technicians. Special packaging is required, and the amount to be shipped is regulated. An FD-861 form (Mail/Package Alert) is required for shipping bomb components to the FBI Laboratory.

Explosives Residue Examinations

Instrumental analyses of explosives residue can determine whether substances are high-explosive, low-explosive, or incendiary mixtures; whether the composition of the substances is consistent with known explosives products; and the type of explosives. Explosives residue can be deposited on metal, plastic, wood, paper, glass, cloth, and other surfaces. Residue may be deposited after handling, storing, or initiating an explosive.

Questions concerning explosives residue evidence should be directed to 703-632-7626. Follow the evidence submission directions, including **Requesting Evidence Examinations** and **Packaging and Shipping Evidence**.

- Some explosives residue is water-soluble and must be protected from moisture. Other residue evaporates quickly and must be collected as soon as possible in airtight containers such as metal cans, glass jars, or heat-sealed or resealable nylon or Mylar bags. Ziplock storage bags are not suitable for shipping or storing explosives residue evidence. Do not fill the containers to the top. Pack to prevent breakage.

- Collect and preserve control samples from the blast site.
- Extreme care must be taken to avoid contaminating explosives residue evidence.
- Never store or ship explosives residue evidence with bulk explosive materials.

Never store or ship explosives residue evidence from a crime scene with evidence from a search site.

FBI Disaster Squad

- Assists in printing the deceased at disaster scenes.
- Assists in collecting antemortem fingerprints of victims.
- Assists in identifying friction ridge skin of the deceased.
- Deployment of the FBI's Disaster Squad requires consent from the disaster scene coroner or medical examiner, a ranking law enforcement or government official, a representative of the National Transportation Safety Board, or a representative of the US Department of State.
- Requests for assistance must be made through the nearest FBI field office or the FBI's Strategic Information and Operations Center at **202-323-3300.**

Feather Examinations

Feather examinations can determine bird species and can compare feathers found on clothing, vehicles, and other objects with feathers from the crime scene.

Questions concerning feather evidence should be directed to 703-632-8449. Follow the evidence submission directions, including **Requesting Evidence Examinations** and **Packaging and Shipping Evidence**.

- Submit feathers in heat-sealed or resealable plastic bags or paper bags.

Firearm Examinations

Firearms

Firearm examinations can determine the general condition of a firearm and whether the firearm is mechanically functional or in a condition that could contribute to an unintentional discharge. Trigger-pull examinations can determine the amount of pressure necessary to release the hammer or firing pin of a firearm. Examinations can determine whether a firearm was altered to fire in the full-automatic mode. Obliterated and/or altered firearm serial numbers sometimes can be restored. Firearms can be test-fired to obtain known specimens for comparison with evidence ammunition components, such as bullets, cartridge cases, and shotshell casings.

Comparisons of suspect firearms can be made with firearms depicted in surveillance images, possibly resulting in an "association" conclusion. Photogrammetry can determine the length of the weapon(s) used by the subject(s) depicted in the surveillance images. See **Image Analysis Examinations**.

Bullets

Fired bullets can be examined to determine general rifling characteristics such as caliber, physical features of the rifling impressions, and the manufacturer of the bullets. The microscopic characteristics on evidence bullets can be compared with test-fired bullets from a suspect firearm to determine whether the evidence bullet was fired from that firearm.

Cartridge Cases or Shotshell Casings

Cartridge-case or shotshell-casing examinations can determine the caliber or gauge, the manufacturer, and whether there are marks of value for comparison. The images of questioned cartridge cases and shotshell casings can be scanned into the National Integrated Ballistic Information Network (NIBIN) to compare with evidence from other shooting incidents. The microscopic characteristics of evidence cartridge cases and shotshell casings can be examined to determine whether they were fired from a specific firearm.

Shot Pellets, Buckshot, or Slugs

Examinations of shot pellets, buckshot, or slugs can determine the size of the shot, the gauge of the slug, and the manufacturer.

Wadding

Examinations of wadding components can determine the gauge and the manufacturer.

Unfired Cartridges or Shotshells

Examinations of unfired cartridges or shotshells can determine the caliber or gauge and whether there are marks of value for comparison. Examinations also can determine whether the ammunition was loaded in and extracted from a specific firearm. Unfired and fired cartridges or shotshells can be associated through manufacturing marks.

Gunshot Residue on Victim's Clothing

The deposition of gunshot residue on evidence such as clothing varies with the distance from the muzzle of the firearm to the target. Patterns of gunshot residue can be duplicated using a questioned firearm-and-ammunition combination fired into test materials at known distances. These patterns serve as a basis for estimating muzzle-to-garment distances.

Gun Parts

Examinations of gun parts can determine the caliber and model of the gun from which the parts originated.

Silencers

Muzzle attachments can reduce the noise of a firearm by suppressing sound during firing. Testing can determine whether a muzzle attachment can be classified as a silencer based on a measurable sound-reduction capability.

Questions concerning firearm evidence should be directed to 703-632-8442. Follow the evidence submission directions, including **Requesting Evidence Examinations** and **Packaging and Shipping Evidence**.

- All firearms must be unloaded.
- The firearm should be submitted. If the firearm cannot be submitted, call **703-632-8442** for instructions.
- The firearm must be handled minimally to avoid loss or destruction of evidence. Do not allow objects to enter or contact the firearm's barrel, chamber, or other operating surface.
- Firearms and ammunition components such as bullets, cartridge cases, and shotshell casings can be sent via Registered Mail through the US Postal Service. Evidence must be packaged separately and identified

by date, time, location, collector's name, case number, and evidence number.

- US Department of Transportation regulations and the following guidelines must be followed when **shipping live ammunition**:
  - Package and ship ammunition separately from firearm(s).
  - The outside of the container must be labeled "ORM-D, CARTRIDGES, SMALL ARMS".
  - The Declaration of Dangerous Goods must include the number of package(s) and the gross weight in grams of the completed package(s).
- Do not mark the firearm. Firearms must be identified with a tag containing the caliber, make, model, and serial number. The date, time, name(s) of the owner(s), location, collector's name, case number, and evidence number must be on the container.
- Do not mark bullets, cartridges and cartridge cases, shotshells and shotshell casings, or other firearm-related evidence. The date, time, location, collector's name, case number, and evidence number must be on the container.
- Clothing submitted for gunshot residue examination must be carefully handled, air-dried, and wrapped separately in paper. Clothing with blood must be air-dried and labeled "BIOHAZARD" on the inner and outer containers. The date, time, location, collector's name, case number, and evidence number must be on the container.

Forensic Facial Imaging

Visual information specialists provide composite drawings, two- and three-dimensional facial reconstructions from skeletal remains, facial age progressions, postmortem reconstructions, and digital photographic manipulations and retouches. Interviews required to prepare composite drawings may be conducted either by having a visual information specialist travel to the field or by using video teleconferencing.

For facial comparisons between known and questioned subjects, see **Image Analysis Examinations**.

Questions concerning forensic facial imaging should be directed to 703-632-8194.

Glass Examinations

Glass comparison examinations can determine whether particles of glass originated from a broken source of glass. Glass fracture examinations can determine the direction and type of the breaking force and the sequencing of shots.

Questions concerning glass evidence should be directed to 703-632-8449. Follow the evidence submission directions, including **Requesting Evidence Examinations** and **Packaging and Shipping Evidence**.

Comparison

- Submit samples of glass from each broken window or source in leak-proof containers such as film canisters or plastic pill bottles. Do not use paper or glass containers.
- Submit samples of laminated glass (e.g., windshield) from each side of the glass. Label the samples "INSIDE" and "OUTSIDE" and package separately in leak-proof containers such as film canisters or plastic pill bottles. Do not use paper or glass containers.
- Submit the air-dried clothing of the victim(s) and suspect(s). Package each item separately in a paper bag.

- Search for particles in the hair, skin, and wounds of the victim(s) and suspect(s). Submit particles in leak-proof containers such as film canisters or plastic pill bottles. Do not use paper or glass containers.
- Search for particles in vehicles by vacuuming each section of the vehicle separately. Do not use tape for recovering glass particles. Submit vacuum sweepings in leak-proof containers. Do not use paper or glass containers.
- Ship known and questioned debris separately to avoid contamination.
- Do not process evidence for latent prints.

Fracture

- Label the sides of the glass in the frame ("INSIDE" and "OUTSIDE"). Label the glass where it was removed in the frame ("TOP," "BOTTOM," "LEFT", and "RIGHT").
- Submit all glass pieces so that the pieces can be fit together to identify the radial cracks near and at the point(s) of impact and to increase the probability of matching edges. Pack all glass separately and securely to avoid shifting and breaking during shipping.
- Submit the entire piece of laminated glass, if possible. Secure the glass between sheets of plywood or sturdy cardboard. Do not place any objects into the impact area.

Do not process evidence for latent prints.

Hair and Fiber Examinations

Hair

Hair examinations can determine whether hairs are animal or human. Race, body area, method of removal, damage, and alteration (e.g., bleaching or dyeing) can be determined from human-hair analysis. Examinations can associate a hair to a person on the basis of microscopic characteristics in the hair but cannot provide absolute personal identification. Hairs that are associated will be submitted for mitochondrial DNA analysis.

Fibers

Fiber examinations can identify the type of fiber, such as animal (wool), vegetable (cotton), mineral (glass), and synthetic (manufactured). Questioned fibers can be compared with fibers from the clothing, carpeting, and other textiles of victim(s) and suspect(s). A questioned piece of fabric can be matched physically to known fabric. Fabric composition, construction, and color can be compared, and impressions on and from fabric can be examined. Label searches can determine clothing manufacturer information.

Questions concerning hair and fiber evidence should be directed to 703-632-8449. Follow the evidence submission directions, including **Requesting Evidence Examinations** and **Packaging and Shipping Evidence**.

- For known hair samples, collect at least 25 hairs from different parts of the head and/or pubic region. Comb and pull out the hairs. Submit hairs in clean paper or an envelope with sealed corners.
- When possible, submit the entire garment or textile. Submit fibers in clean paper or an envelope with sealed corners.

Image Analysis Examinations

Image analysis examinations are conducted by the FBI's Operational Technology Division (OTD), Digital Evidence Laboratory (DEL), Forensic Audio, Video, and Image Analysis Unit (FAVIAU).

The OTD DEL has different acceptance criteria and a different physical address than the FBI Laboratory, as described below.

Photographic Comparisons

Examinations of film, negatives, digital images, photographic prints, and video recordings, including surveillance images, involve comparisons of subject(s) or object(s) depicted in questioned images with those in known images. Subject(s) or object(s) also can be compared between multiple questioned images. Subject comparisons include facial comparisons or can be made between like body parts, such as hands or ears. Examples of objects that can be compared include clothing, firearms, and vehicles.

Photogrammetry

Physical dimensions can be derived from images through the use of geometric formulas or on-site comparison. For on-site comparisons, examiners enter the scene and place a height chart at the location of the subject(s) or object(s) of interest. Examples of photogrammetry include determining the height of a bank robbery subject(s) and the length of the weapon(s) used by the subject(s) depicted in surveillance images.

Authenticity and Image-manipulation Detection

Photographic evidence—including film, video, and digital images—can be examined to determine whether the image is the result of a composite, an alteration, or a copy.

Location, Time, and Date

Examinations of photographic evidence can determine the location, time, and date that an image was taken.

Source and Age

Photographic products, including film and prints, can be dated, and the source can be established by examining manufacturing characteristics. This can establish the time frame during which a photograph was taken.

Cameras

Cameras, both film and digital, seized as evidence can be compared with images to determine whether a specific camera captured a specific image. Similarly, digital video cameras can be compared with video clips.

Video

Still images can be produced from video clips, enhanced and enlarged, and used in courtroom presentations.

Automobile Make and Model Identification

Vehicles depicted in surveillance images can be compared with the National Automotive Image File to determine make and model.

Child Pornography Examinations

Seized images of child pornography should be searched for known victims by checking with the National Center for Missing and Exploited Children and the Innocent Images National Initiative. The images also can be compared with images in the Child Exploitation and Obscenity Reference File to identify the source of the images. Video clips can be examined to determine if any of the people and scenes depicted in the video clips are also recorded as still images in the reference file. Video clips and still images also can be examined to determine if they depict recordings or images of real people and events or whether they represent computer-generated subjects and events.

Questions concerning image analysis examinations should be directed to 703-985-1393. Questions

concerning image analysis evidence should be directed to 703-985-1388.

Image analysis examinations may not be submitted directly from entities outside the FBI.

State, local, or international agency cases must be submitted by the FBI field office servicing the area and must meet one of the following two criteria: 1) the state, local, or international case has a nexus to an ongoing FBI investigation or 2) the FBI division head deems that the case is of enough regional importance to merit the dedication of federal resources to the state, local, or international case. These criteria shall be met with a written statement from the division head (Special Agent in Charge). FBI entities may submit cases directly.

Follow the evidence submission directions, including **Requesting Evidence Examinations** and **Packaging and Shipping Evidence**.

- Write-protect the original media. Never use the Pause operation when viewing original video recordings.
- Submit original evidence (e.g., negatives, videotape, CD) whenever possible because it contains the greatest level of detail. If the original media is unavailable, submit first-generation photographic prints, videotapes, or digital files of the evidence, being careful not to introduce further compression.
- Process all film prior to submitting. Bank surveillance film should be processed by the bank's security company according to manufacturer specifications.
- When requesting forensic examinations based on video images, queue the original videotape to the approximate time of the pertinent area. State in a communication the date and time of the pertinent area and use the date-time stamp on the images or

the counter indicator (set from the beginning of the tape at 000). If prints from the relevant frames are available, submit them for reference.

- Arrest or known photographs of suspect(s) for comparison with questioned images must depict the suspect(s) from many angles similar to the questioned images. If a facial comparison is requested, ensure that the face or head of the suspect(s) fills more than half the frame. If questioned images show tattoos or marks, include photographs of the same areas of the body on the known suspect(s).
- When taking known photographs for comparison with questioned images, use 35 mm film or digital equivalent (at highest resolution settings to minimize image compression).
- Do not mark or cut items submitted for comparison (e.g., clothing or firearms) where they are visible in the questioned images.
- Physical items such as clothing and firearms must be submitted to the Laboratory for other examinations such as trace evidence, ballistic, or fingerprint analyses before they are submitted for image comparison.
- If photogrammetry is requested, include the dimensions of the scene to the nearest eighth of an inch and include a diagram or print from the relevant images indicating the location of the measurements. Include one diagram or print for every angle used in the scene. Do not touch or move the surveillance cameras.
- Submissions for comparison with the Child Exploitation and Obscenity Reference File must be limited to no more than 30 images. Call **703-985-1393** for specific instructions.

- When submitting such evidence as a videotape or data card, label the outer container "FRAGILE, SENSITIVE ELECTRONIC EQUIPMENT" or "FRAGILE, SENSITIVE AUDIO/VIDEO MEDIA" and "KEEP AWAY FROM MAGNETS OR MAGNETIC FIELDS".
- Address the outer container as follows:

Forensic Program, Building - 27958A, Engineering Research Facility, Federal Bureau of Investigation, Quantico - VA 22135

Ink Examinations

Examining inked writing in conjunction with other techniques (e.g., handwriting analysis, watermark identification) can provide details regarding document preparation. The composition of writing inks varies with the type of writing instrument (e.g., ballpoint pen, fountain pen, porous-tip pen) and the date of the ink manufacture. In general, inks are composed of dyes in solvents and other materials that impart selected characteristics. Ink analysis usually is limited to comparisons of the organic dye components. When ink formulations are the same, it is not possible to determine whether the ink originated from the same source to the exclusion of others. Examinations cannot determine how long ink has been on a document.

Questions concerning ink evidence should be directed to 703-632-8441. Follow the evidence submission directions, including **Requesting Evidence Examinations** and **Packaging and Shipping Evidence**.

- Pack ink evidence separately from any document or surface with ink marks.

Latent Print Examinations

Case Acceptance Policy

Because of the increasing casework demands of the FBI's primary mission, protecting the United States from terrorist attacks, the FBI Laboratory will no longer accept routine cases from state and local agencies in which latent print examination services may be obtained from within the submitting agency's system. The future acceptance of any state and local cases generally will be based on the submitting agency's lack of access to the same techniques or services provided by the FBI Laboratory, the unusual technical nature of the case, or the circumstances surrounding the case, e.g., cases of a high-profile nature or cases that also involve FBI field offices.

Developing Latent Prints at Crime Scenes

The Laboratory is the best place to develop latent prints; however, it is sometimes necessary to develop latent prints at crime scenes. Caution should be taken to prevent destroying latent prints. The following measures ensure that crime scene latent prints are protected:

- Photograph latent prints prior to any processing.
- Examine all evidence visually and with a laser or an alternate light source before using any other latent print development process.
- Photograph latent prints developed with fingerprint powders before lifting them.
- Black, gray, or white powder can be applied to a surface with a variety of style of brushes. The color of the powder should contrast with the color of the surface (e.g., black for light surfaces and gray or white for dark surfaces).

- Use a short-hair brush or cotton to remove excess powder. Use caution when powdering. Avoid overbrushing latent prints and losing clarity.
- Use transparent tape or black-and-white rubber lifts to lift latent prints.
- When transparent tape is used, the color of the backing card should contrast with the color of the powders (e.g., white backing card for black powder).
- When using latent print development processes, refer to the manufacturer's instructions and the Material Safety Data Sheets. Use personal protective equipment (e.g., safety glasses, masks, gloves, smocks).
- The *Processing Guide for Developing Latent Prints* is a comprehensive guide to latent print processes and protocols. Refer to this publication to ensure that proper processes are applied in the recommended order. Following this guide will maximize the potential to develop latent prints and will preserve evidence if other forensic examinations are required. The guide is available at **http://www.fbi.gov/hq/lab/fsc/backissu/jan2001/lpu.pdf**. Law enforcement personnel may request the *Processing Guide for Developing Latent Prints* in field-manual format by faxing a request on agency letterhead to **703-632-8374.**

Photographing Latent Prints

- Use a tripod and cable release when photographing latent prints.
- Use a 35 mm or medium-format camera with a macro lens capable of half-size to full-size reproduction.
- Photograph latent prints at each step in the processing sequence before moving to the next process.

- Photograph latent prints developed with fingerprint powders before lifting them.

When possible, use ISO 400 film. Set the lens f-stop to the smallest possible aperture while using the camera meter to adjust the camera's shutter speed to obtain proper exposure.

Take three exposures of each latent print by bracketing:

  - Original exposure.
  - One-stop underexposed image.
  - One-stop overexposed image.

- Photograph latent prints individually. This ensures that the target latent print is in focus.
- For reference purposes, photograph latent prints close to one another in one frame, if possible.
- Fill the frame completely.
- Photograph latent prints with an identification label that includes a scale, reference number, date, collector's initials, and location of the latent prints. The identification label should be placed on the same plane as the latent prints.
- Maintain a photographic log that records each shot, reference number, date, collector's initials, location of prints, and other pertinent information.

Questions concerning latent print evidence should be directed to 703-632-8443. Follow the evidence submission directions, including **Requesting Evidence Examinations** and **Packaging and Shipping Evidence**.

- Stabilize the evidence to avoid movement or friction during shipping.
- Place non-porous evidence (e.g., non-absorbent, hard surfaces) in separate protective coverings such as

thick transparent envelopes (glassine), or suspend in a container so that there is minimal surface contact. Friction will destroy latent prints on this type of surface.

- Place porous evidence (e.g., paper, cardboard) in separate protective coverings. Friction generally will not destroy latent prints on this type of surface.
- Submit known fingerprints and palm prints of everyone who may have handled the evidence, including suspects, victims, those who had legitimate access, and investigative personnel. All fingerprint cards must include pertinent biographical and/or demographic information.
- Palm prints should be taken on only one side of a separate card, not on the reverse side of a fingerprint card or on the reverse side of a card that has a recorded impression on the other side.
- Fingerprint cards and major-case prints should include, at a minimum, the name of the person printed, the name of the person recording the prints, the date, the case-identification number, and a brief statement of facts relating to the case. The fingerprint card should bear an arrest offense.
- The notation "elimination prints" should be included if the person printed is not a suspect.
- When known prints are submitted separately from evidence, reference previous communications and case-identifying numbers and other pertinent information.

Submitting Latent and Intentionally Recorded Print Images in Digital Format

Digital images, including digital photographs, of latent and intentionally recorded prints should include a scale or other measurable item. If a search of the Integrated Automated Fingerprint Identification System (IAFIS) is requested, a scale or other measurable item is mandatory.

Digital images, including digital photographs, must meet the following requirements:

- Documentation of the image source (e.g., window, door frame).
- Documentation of the capture device (e.g., flatbed scanner, digital camera).
- Documentation indicating the image is an original capture.
- File properties for latent images consisting of:
    - A file format without compression or with lossless compression (e.g., RAW, TIFF).
    - A minimum of 8 bits for grayscale images and 24 bits for color images.
    - A resolution that meets or exceeds 1000 pixels per inch (PPI) when calibrated to actual size (1:1).
- File properties for intentionally recorded prints consisting of:
    - A file format without compression, with lossless compression (e.g., RAW, TIFF), or with Wavelet Scalar Quantization (WSQ) compression saved at a maximum of 15:1.
    - A minimum of 8 bits for grayscale images and 24 bits for color images.
    - A resolution that meets or exceeds 500 PPI when calibrated to actual size (1:1).

Latent prints submitted as facsimiles or photocopies will not be examined in the FBI Laboratory.

Intentionally recorded prints submitted as facsimiles will not be examined in the FBI Laboratory, except when the known prints will be searched against IAFIS in order to obtain FBI file prints.

Submitting Hands or Fingers of an Unknown Deceased

- Pack each hand or finger in a separate unbreakable, watertight, and airtight container.
- Label each container (e.g., "RIGHT HAND," "RIGHT THUMB," "RIGHT INDEX").
- Ship the remains in the condition in which they were found (e.g., in water, frozen, dried) by the most expeditious means.
- Provide a complete physical description of the deceased, if possible.
- Label the outer container "KEEP IN A COOL, DRY PLACE", "REFRIGERATE ON ARRIVAL", and "BIOHAZARD".
- All human remains will be returned to the contributor.
- Address the outer container as follows:

Evidence Control Unit, Laboratory Division, Federal Bureau of Investigation, 2501 Investigation Parkway, Quantico VA 22135

Legible, complete ten-print fingerprint cards not related to an ongoing Laboratory investigation should be sent to the FBI's Criminal Justice Information Services Division.

- Address the outer container as follows:

**CRIMINAL JUSTICE INFORMATION SERVICES DIVISION
FEDERAL BUREAU OF INVESTIGATION
1000, CUSTER HOLLOW ROAD
CLARKSBURG WV 26306**

- Questions concerning ten-print fingerprint cards should be directed to 304-625-2360.

Lubricant Examinations

Lubricants encompass a range of substances, including petroleum products, natural fatty ester oils, and polyalkylene glycol oils. Automotive fluids (e.g., engine oil, brake fluid), certain cosmetics (e.g., bath oils, lotions), and some polishes contain lubricants. Lubricant examinations may also be conducted in sexual assault, vehicular homicide, or heavy-equipment sabotage cases.

Questions concerning lubricant evidence should be directed to 703-632-8441. Follow the evidence submission directions, including **Requesting Evidence Examinations** and **Packaging and Shipping Evidence**.

- Submit entire items (e.g., clothing) when possible. Air-dry the evidence, and package separately in paper bags.
- Absorb suspected lubricants onto a clean cotton cloth or swab. Leave a portion of the cloth or swab unstained as a control. Air-dry the swab and pack in a heat-sealed or resealable plastic bag.
- Submit suspected sources of lubricants for comparison examinations.
- Package lubricants separately in leak-proof containers.

Metallurgy Examinations

Comparison

Comparative examinations can determine whether two metals or metallic objects came from the same source or from each other. Metal comparisons can identify various surface and microstructural characteristics—including fractured areas, accidental damage, and fabrication marks—to determine whether the objects share a common origin. Moreover, the manufacturing methods used to produce an object can be determined. These manufacturing techniques can include casting, forging, hot and cold rolling, extrusion, drawing, swaging, milling, grinding, spinning, blanking, ironing, deep drawing, and others. Examinations can determine mechanical properties, such as the response of a metal to an applied force or load. Examinations also can determine chemical composition, including alloying and trace elements.

Broken or Mechanically Damaged Metal

The causes of failure or damage—such as the application of stress exceeding the tensile strength or yield limit of the metal; a material or manufacturing defect; or corrosion, cracking, or excessive service usage (fatigue)—can be determined. The magnitude of the force or load that caused the failure, how the force or load was transmitted to the metal, and the direction it was transmitted also can be determined.

Burned, Heated, or Melted Metal

Examinations can determine the approximate temperature to which a metal was exposed, the nature of the heat source, and whether a metal was in an electrical short-circuit situation.

Cut or Severed Metal

Examinations can determine the method by which a metal was severed, such as sawing, shearing, milling, turning, or thermal cutting. The nature of the thermal source (e.g., burner bar, electric arc welder) used can sometimes be determined.

Metal Fragments

Examinations can determine how metal fragments were formed. If fragments were formed by impulsive (short-duration, high strain rate) loading, an examination can determine whether an explosive was detonated and the magnitude of the detonation velocity. The nature of the object that was the source of the fragments often can be determined as well.

Specification Fraud and Non-compliant Materials

Metallurgical testing of materials can determine whether inferior components were substituted in contracting frauds. The composition and mechanical properties of materials can be examined to determine if the components meet contractual obligations or appropriate regulatory codes. Precious-metal content also can be determined.

Lamp Bulbs

Examinations can determine whether a lamp bulb was incandescent when its glass envelope was broken. Determinations also can be made as to whether a lamp bulb was incandescent when it was subjected to an impact force such as a vehicular collision. Such determinations can be made even if the glass was broken by the impact.

Watches, Clocks, and Timers

The conditions causing a watch, clock, timer, or other mechanism to stop or malfunction and whether the time displayed represents a.m. or p.m. (calendar-type timing mechanisms only) can be determined. The on/off condition of appliance timers damaged by a fire or explosion often can be determined.

Objects with Questioned Internal Components

X-ray radiography can non-destructively reveal the interior construction and the presence or absence of defects, cavities, or foreign materials. The position of on/off switches and other mechanical components can be determined.

Questions concerning metallurgy evidence should be directed to 703-632-8441. Follow the evidence submission directions, including **Requesting Evidence Examinations** and **Packaging and Shipping Evidence**.

National Missing Person DNA Database Program Examinations

The National Missing Person DNA Database (NMPDD) Program is supported by both the DNA Analysis Unit I (DNAUI) and DNA Analysis Unit II (DNAUII). Nuclear DNA examinations are conducted in the DNAUI and mitochondrial DNA examinations are conducted in the DNAUII to support the NMPDD Program. Each unit has an NMPDD Program Manager who is available to answer any questions regarding case submission (contact information is listed below). Local, state, and federal law enforcement missing-person cases can be submitted directly to the FBI Laboratory or through the FBI field offices or resident agencies. All agencies must contact one of the FBI Laboratory's NMPDD Program Managers before submitting samples. The submitting agency must have the necessary information and completed forms for sample submission. The FBI will perform mitochondrial DNA and nuclear DNA (STR) analyses on samples.

All samples submitted to the FBI Laboratory must have an incoming letter describing the samples submitted. A copy of the anthropology, odontology (dental), medical examiner and/or coroner, and law enforcement reports must be included with unidentified human remains samples submitted.

Contact either of the NMPDD Program Managers prior to submitting samples or for questions concerning samples.

- Call **703-632-7586** for the DNAUI or **703-632-7582** for the DNAUII.
- For FBI (internal) e-mail, write to Eric Pokorak for the DNAUI or John E Stewart for the DNAUII.
- For Internet e-mail, write to **eric.pokorak@ic.fbi.gov** for the DNAUI or **john.stewart@ic.fbi.gov** for the DNAUII.

Follow the evidence submission directions, including **Requesting Evidence Examinations** and **Packaging and Shipping Evidence**.

Samples from Biological Relatives of Missing Persons

- Samples must be sent with a Consent and Information Form for the National Missing Person DNA Database (FD-935 form). A copy of the law enforcement report should accompany the samples submitted.
- Collect samples in the following order of preference:

  1. Dried bloodstains.
  2. Buccal (oral) swabs.

Dried Bloodstains

Use the blood-cell collection kits that are available in FBI field offices or by contacting the NMPDD Program Managers at **703-632-7582** or **703-632-7586**.

Buccal (Oral) Swabs

- Use sterile, cotton-tipped applicator swabs to collect four buccal (oral) samples. Rub the inside surfaces of the cheeks thoroughly (use two swabs on each side).

- Air-dry the swabs and place them back into the original packaging or an envelope with sealed corners. Do not use plastic containers.
- Identify each sample with the date, time, subject's name, location, collector's name, and case number.
- Buccal samples do not need to be refrigerated.

Samples from Unidentified Human Remains

Call the Laboratory prior to submitting bones, teeth, or tissue. The communication accompanying the evidence must reference the telephone conversation accepting the evidence.

Skeletal Samples

Anthropological examinations can determine whether skeletal remains are human or animal. Race, sex, approximate height, and stature at death can be determined from human remains.

- Pick up samples with gloved hands or clean forceps.
- Air-dry samples and place in paper bags.
- Submit whole samples. Cutting skeletal samples increases the possibility of contamination.
- If possible, submit three samples.
- Submit skeletal samples with an anthropological report, preferably from an anthropologist certified by the American Board of Forensic Anthropology, or a medical examiner's/coroner's report.
- Submit skeletal samples in the following order of preference:

  1. Femur.
  2. Tibia.
  3. Humerus.

4. Teeth, skull, and/or mandible.
5. Hand and foot bones.
6. Lower arm bone.
7. Vertebrae.
8. Ribs.

Teeth

Personal identifications can be made by comparing teeth with dental records and X-rays.

- Pick up teeth with gloved hands or clean forceps.
- Air-dry teeth and place in paper bags.
- Submit teeth with an odontological report, preferably from an odontologist certified by the American Board of Forensic Odontology, or a medical examiner's/ coroner's report.
- Submit teeth in the following order of preference:
  1. Non-restored molar.
  2. Non-restored premolar.
  3. Non-restored canine.
  4. Non-restored front tooth.
  5. Restored molar.
  6. Restored premolar.
  7. Restored canine.
  8. Restored front tooth.

Tissue

Tissue samples usually will provide sufficient quantities of DNA for testing.

- Pick up tissue with gloved hands or clean forceps.
- Collect 1–2 cubic inches of red skeletal muscle.
- Place tissue samples in a clean, airtight plastic container without formalin or formaldehyde and keep refrigerated or frozen.
- Label the outer container "KEEP IN A COOL, DRY PLACE", "REFRIGERATE ON ARRIVAL", and "BIOHAZARD".
- Submit to the Laboratory as soon as possible.

Paint Examinations

The layer structure of a questioned paint sample can be compared with a known source from a suspect. The sequence, relative thickness, color, texture, number, and chemical composition of each of the layers can be compared.

The color, manufacturer, model, and model year of an automobile may be determined from a paint chip. Sourcing automotive paints is limited to factory-applied, original automotive paint.

Paint on safes, vaults, windowsills, and door frames can be transferred to and from tools. A comparison can be made between the paint from an object and the paint on a tool.

The Laboratory will not examine evidence to authenticate fine art or historical artifacts or to source spray paint or architectural paints.

Questions concerning paint evidence should be directed to 703-632-8441. Follow the evidence submission directions, including **Requesting Evidence Examinations** and **Packaging and Shipping Evidence**.

- Search the accident or crime scene and the personal effects of the victim(s) to locate paint fragments. Paint fragments often are found in the clothing of the hit-and-run victim(s). Submit the clothing. Paints can be transferred from one car to another, from car to object, or from object to car during an accident or a crime.
- Control paint chips must be collected from the suspected source of the evidentiary paint. Controls must be taken from an area close to, but not in, any damaged area. If no damage is obvious, controls should be taken from several areas of the suspect substrate. Each layer can be a point of comparison. Controls must have all of the layers of paint to the substrate. This can be accomplished by the following:
- Section an area of the painted surface.
- Cut a paint sample from the surface using a clean, sharp instrument.
- Lift or pry loosely attached chips or dislodge the paint by gently hitting the opposite side of the painted surface.
- Package paint specimens in leak-proof containers such as vials or pillboxes. Do not attach paint particles to adhesive tape. Do not use plastic bags, cotton, or envelopes to package paint specimens.

Pepper-spray or Pepper-foam Examinations

Oleoresin capsicum is a resin in various peppers. It may be used in self-defense sprays or foams. Ultra-violet dye (orange) and/or tear gas also may be in the sprays or foams. Items can be analyzed for the presence of oleoresin capsicum, dye, or tear gas.

Questions concerning pepper-spray evidence should be directed to 703-632-8441. Follow the evidence submission directions, including **Requesting Evidence Examinations** and **Packaging and Shipping Evidence**.

- Submit entire items (e.g., clothing) when possible. Air-dry the evidence, and package separately in paper bags.
- Moisten a clean cotton cloth or swab with isopropanol (rubbing alcohol), and wipe over the suspected sprays or foams. Prepare a second moistened cloth or swab as a control. Air-dry the cloths or swabs and pack separately in heat-sealed or resealable plastic bags.
- Submit spray canisters when possible.
- Refer to **Hazardous Materials Transportation** when submitting pepper-spray canisters.

Pharmaceutical Examinations

Pharmaceutical examinations can identify constituents, active ingredients, quantity, and weight.

- **Questions concerning pharmaceutical evidence should be directed to 703-632-8441.** Follow the evidence submission directions, including **Requesting Evidence Examinations** and **Packaging and Shipping Evidence**.
- List the names of the pharmaceuticals and information on their use.
- If possible, submit pharmaceuticals in original containers.

Polymer Examinations

Polymer evidence typically consists of pieces of plastic or other manufactured materials. The source, use, or manufacturer of polymer evidence usually cannot be identified by compositional analysis.

Motor vehicle trim can be compared with plastic remaining on property struck in a hit-and-run case. The manufacturer, make, model, and model year of a vehicle can be determined if a manufacturer's part number is on the trim.

Plastics in wire insulation and miscellaneous plastics such as buttons can be compared with known sources.

Questions concerning polymer evidence should be directed to 703-632-8441. Follow the evidence submission directions, including **Requesting Evidence Examinations** and **Packaging and Shipping Evidence**.

- When a motor vehicle has been in an accident, fragments (e.g., plastic lens covers) can be left at the scene. These pieces can be physically reconstructed with the remnants of the fixture left on the car. Collect and package the fragments carefully to keep the edges intact.
- Search the accident or crime scene and personal effects of the victim(s) to locate plastic fragments. Submit fragments in leakproof containers such as film canisters or plastic pill bottles. Do not use cotton or paper containers.
- Remove damaged suspect motor vehicle parts, and package separately in resealable plastic bags or boxes.
- If possible, submit entire items (e.g., clothing) with potential or smeared polymeric transfers. Package separately in paper bags. If the entire item cannot be submitted, cut with a clean, sharp instrument a section where the transfer is suspected. Collect an unstained control sample. Pack to prevent stain removal by abrasive action during shipping. Pack in clean paper. Do not use plastic containers.

Product-tampering Examinations

Product-tampering is when a commercial product is intentionally distorted to harm someone or to extort money or other thing of value. Examples range from drug-tampering in medical environments, food adulteration in supermarkets, and the combination of tampering and altering in domestic settings.

The Laboratory will not assess manufacturing quality control or product specifications in commercial products.

Questions concerning product-tampering evidence should be directed to 703-632-8441. Follow the evidence submission directions, including **Requesting Evidence Examinations** and **Packaging and Shipping Evidence**.

- Submit control samples of the unadulterated product.
- Package and ship control and suspect samples separately to avoid contamination. Submit samples in leak-proof containers such as film canisters or plastic pill bottles. Do not use paper or glass containers.
- Use caution to prevent the destruction of latent prints.

Questioned Document Examinations

Handwriting and Hand Printing

The examination and comparison of handwriting characteristics can determine the origin or authenticity of questioned writing, although not all handwriting is identifiable with a specific writer. Intent and such traits as age, sex, and personality cannot be determined from handwriting examinations. Some reasons for inconclusive results include:

- Limited questioned and/or known writing.
- Lack of sufficiently comparable known writing for comparison.

- Lack of contemporaneous writing or lapse of time between execution of questioned and known writing.
- Distortion or disguise in the questioned and/or known writing.
- Lack of sufficient identifying characteristics.
- Submission of photocopied evidence instead of original evidence.

Procedures for Obtaining Known Writing Exemplars

- The text, size of paper, space available for writing, writing instrument, and writing style (handwriting or hand printing) must be as close to the original writing as possible.
- Give verbal or typewritten instructions concerning the text to be written. Do not give instructions on spelling, punctuation, or arrangement of writing.
- All exemplars must be on separate pieces of paper.

  The writer and witness must initial and date each page of writing.
- Do not allow the writer to see the previous exemplars or the questioned writing. Remove each exemplar from the writer's sight as soon as it is completed.
- Numerous repetitions may be necessary to obtain naturally prepared writing.
- Obtain exemplars from the right and left hands.
- Obtain hand-printing exemplars in upper- and lowercase letters.
- Obtain a sufficient quantity of exemplars to account for natural variation in the writing.

- Obtain undictated writing such as business records, personal correspondence, and cancelled checks or other documents prepared during the normal course of business activity.

Common Types of Non-genuine Signatures

- Traced signatures are prepared by directly using a genuine signature as a template or pattern.
- Simulated signatures are prepared by copying or drawing a genuine signature.
- Freehand signatures are written in the forger's normal handwriting with no attempt to copy another's writing style. Therefore, it may be possible to identify the writer(s) who prepared the signature(s).

Altered or Obliterated Writing

Documents can be examined for the presence of altered or obliterated writing, and the original writing may be deciphered.

Typewriting

Questioned typewriting may be identified with the typewriter that produced it. This is most common when the typewriter is a typebar machine. The identification is based on individual characteristics that develop during the manufacturing process and through use and abuse of the typewriter.

Typewriters with interchangeable elements (e.g., ball, printwheel, or thimble) are less likely to be associated with questioned typewriting. However, these typing elements may be positively identified with specific texts by examining individual characteristics of the elements.

Comparison of questioned typewriting with reference standards can determine a possible make and model of the typewriter and/or the typewriter elements.

Carbon-film typewriter ribbons and correction ribbons retain readable text. These ribbons can be compared with questioned typewritten impressions. Generally, fabric ribbons cannot be read or identified.

Procedures for Obtaining Known Typewriting Exemplars

- If the typewriter has a carbon-film ribbon or correction ribbon, remove it from the typewriter and submit the ribbon to the Laboratory. Insert a new ribbon in the typewriter prior to obtaining exemplars.
- If the typewriter has a fabric ribbon, remove it from the typewriter and put the typewriter in the stencil position. Place a sheet of carbon paper over a sheet of blank paper and insert both into the typewriter. Allow the typeface to strike the carbon paper. Submit the fabric ribbon and the exemplars typed on the carbon paper to the Laboratory.
- Obtain two full word-for-word typed exemplars of the questioned text and two typed exemplars of the entire keyboard (all symbols, numbers, and upper- and lowercase letters).
- Record the make, model, and serial number of the typewriter on the exemplars. Also record the date the exemplars were obtained and the name of the person who typed the exemplars.
- Obtain the typewriter service and repair history, if available.
- Normally, it is not necessary to send the typewriter to the Laboratory; however, in some cases, the examiner will request the typewriter. It must be packed securely to prevent damage during shipment. Typewriter elements (e.g., ball, printwheel, or thimble) also must be submitted to the Laboratory.

Photocopies or Facsimiles

Photocopies or facsimiles of documents can be identified with the machine used to produce them if the exemplars and questioned documents are relatively contemporaneous. The possible make and model of the photocopier or facsimile machine sometimes can be determined.

Procedures for Obtaining Known Photocopy Exemplars

- Obtain at least 10 exemplars without a document on the glass plate and with the cover down.
- Obtain at least 10 exemplars without a document on the glass plate and with the cover up.
- Obtain at least 10 exemplars with a document on the glass plate and the cover down.
- Obtain at least 10 exemplars with a document through the automatic document feeder, if applicable.
- Record on each exemplar the date the exemplars were obtained, the name of the person who prepared the exemplars, and the conditions under which the exemplars were made.
- Record the make, model, and serial number of the photocopier; information about the toner supplies and components; whether the paper supply is sheet- or roll-fed; and options such as color, reduction, enlargement, zoom, mask, trim, and editor board.
- Do not store or ship photocopies in plastic envelopes.

Graphic Arts (Commercial and Office Printing)

Printed documents can be associated with a common source or identified with known commercial printing paraphernalia such as artwork, negatives, and plates or office printing devices such as ink-jet or laser printers.

Paper

Torn edges can be compared. The paper manufacturer can be determined if a watermark is present. Paper can be examined for indented writing. Do not rub the indentations with a pencil. Do not add indentations by writing on top of the evidence.

Burned or Charred Paper

Burned or charred documents (not completely reduced to ash) may be deciphered and stabilized. The document must be handled minimally. The document must be shipped in the container in which it was burned, in polyester film encapsulation, or between layers of cotton in a rigid container.

Age of a Document

The earliest date a document could have been prepared may be determined by examining various physical characteristics, including watermarks, indented writing, printing, typewriting, and inks.

Carbon Paper or Carbon-film Ribbon

Used carbon paper or a carbon-film ribbon can be examined to disclose the content of the text.

Checkwriters

A checkwriter impression can be compared with a known source. Examining checkwriter impressions may determine the brand or model of the checkwriter.

Embossings and Seals

An embossed or seal impression can be compared with a known source. Submit the device to the Laboratory.

Rubber Stamps

A rubber-stamp impression can be compared with a known source. Submit the rubber stamp to the Laboratory uncleaned.

Plastic Bags

Plastic bags (e.g., sandwich and garbage bags) can be compared with a roll or box of bags.

Anonymous Letter File

The Anonymous Letter File contains images of anonymous and/or threatening communications submitted to the Questioned Documents Unit for examination. This file can be searched in an attempt to associate text from a communication in one case with text from communications in other cases.

Bank Robbery Note File

The Bank Robbery Note File contains images of notes used in bank robberies. This file can be searched in an attempt to associate text from one bank robbery note with text from bank robbery notes in other cases.

Questions concerning documentary evidence should be directed to 703-632-8444. Follow the evidence submission directions, including **Requesting Evidence Examinations** and **Packaging and Shipping Evidence**.

- Documentary evidence must be preserved in the condition in which it was found. It must not be unnecessarily folded, torn, marked, soiled, stamped, or written on or handled excessively. Protect the evidence from inadvertent indented writing. Mark documents unobtrusively by writing the collector's initials, date, and other information in pencil.

- Whenever possible, submit the original evidence to the Laboratory. The lack of detail in photocopies makes examinations difficult and often will result in inconclusive opinions. Copies are sufficient for reference-file searches.
- Do not store or ship photocopies in plastic envelopes.

Rope and Cordage Examinations

A piece of rope or cord can be compared with a questioned rope or cord. The composition, construction, color, and diameter can be determined. If a tracer is present, the manufacturer can be determined.

Questions concerning rope and cordage evidence should be directed to 703-632-8449. Follow the evidence submission directions, including **Requesting Evidence Examinations** and **Packaging and Shipping Evidence**.

- Submit the entire rope or cord. If the rope or cord must be cut, specify which end was cut during evidence collection.
- Label the known and questioned samples.
- Handle the sections of rope or cord carefully to prevent loss of trace material or contamination.
- Submit in heat-sealed or resealable plastic or paper bags.

Safe-insulation Examinations

Safe insulation can be compared to a known source. Examinations of safe insulation sometimes can determine the manufacturer.

Questions concerning safe-insulation evidence should be directed to 703-632-8449. Follow the evidence submission directions, including **Requesting Evidence Examinations** and **Packaging and Shipping Evidence**.

- Collect safe-insulation samples from damaged areas.
- Safe insulation can adhere to people, clothing, tools, bags, and stolen items and can transfer to vehicles. If possible, submit the evidence to the Laboratory for examiners to remove the debris. Package each item of evidence in a separate paper bag. Do not process tools for latent prints.
- Ship known and questioned debris separately to avoid contamination. Submit known and questioned debris in leak-proof containers such as film canisters or plastic pill bottles. Do not use paper or glass containers. Pack to keep lumps intact.

Serial-number Examinations

Obliterated serial or identification numbers—including markings on metal, wood, plastic, and fiberglass—often are restorable. Comparisons can be made with suspect dies.

Questions concerning serial-number evidence should be directed to 703-632-8442. Follow the evidence submission directions, including **Requesting Evidence Examinations** and **Packaging and Shipping Evidence**.

- For large objects, and if possible, remove the section containing the serial number and submit it to the Laboratory.
- If it is not possible to remove the section containing the serial number, make a cast to submit to the Laboratory.
  1. Use an acrylic-surface replica cast kit. Call the Laboratory at **703-632-8442** regarding the appropriate cast kit.
  2. Different formulas are used in different temperatures. If possible, move the evidence to a warm area.

3. Casts will duplicate foreign material in the stamped characters. Clean the area before proceeding. Remove paint and dirt with a solvent such as acetone, gasoline, or paint remover. Use Naval Jelly to remove rust. Use a soft brush. Do not use a wire brush.

4. Build a dam around the stamped characters to retain the acrylic liquid while it hardens. Use a soft and pliable dam material such as modeling clay. Ensure there are no voids in the dam.

5. Following the instructions in the kit, mix the liquid and powder for one minute and pour the mixture into the dam.

6. The acrylic liquid will take 30 minutes to harden. Remove the cast when it is hard. If paint and rust are on the cast, make additional casts and submit the cleanest one to the Laboratory.

7. Indicate from where on the object (often a vehicle) the cast was taken.

8. Pack the cast to prevent breakage.

Shoe Print and Tire Tread Examinations

Shoe print or tire tread impressions are routinely left at crime scenes. These impressions are retained on surfaces in two- and three-dimensional forms. Almost all impressions, including partial impressions, have value for forensic comparisons. The examination of detailed shoe print and tire tread impressions often results in the positive identification of the shoes of the suspect(s) or tire(s) from the vehicle(s) of the suspect(s).

Photographing Shoe Print and Tire Tread Impressions

General crime scene photographs must be taken to relate the impressions to the crime scene. Examination-quality photographs then must be taken to obtain maximum detail for forensic examination and must include a scale. All impressions must be photographed using both methods.

General Crime Scene Photographs

General crime scene photographs of shoe print or tire tread impressions must include close-range and long-range photographs. ISO 400 color film should be used. The photographs must show the relationship of the impressions to the surrounding area. General crime scene photographs are not suitable for footwear or tire examinations.

Examination-quality Photographs

Examination-quality photographs must be taken directly over the impressions using a tripod and lighting. A scale must be in every photograph. The purpose of these photographs is to produce a detailed negative that can be enlarged to natural size. Examination-quality photographs must be taken as follows:

1. Place a linear scale such as a ruler next to and on the same plane as the impression. Place a label in the picture to correlate the impression with crime scene notes and general photographs.

2. Images should be taken using a 35 mm or medium-format film camera. Low-cost digital cameras do not provide sufficient image detail for examination-quality photographs. Use a manual-focus camera. If the shoe print is made from a colored substance (e.g., blood), color film may be preferable to black and white. In most ambient-light situations, use ISO 100 film. Use ISO 200 or 400 film, if necessary.

3. Place the camera on a tripod and position it directly over the impression. Adjust the height of the camera, and if possible, use a normal lens (50 mm

for a 35 mm camera). Fill the frame with the impression and scale. Position the camera so the film plane is parallel to the impression.

4. Set the f-stop on f/16 or f/22 for a greater depth of field.
5. Attach an electronic flash with a long extension cord to the camera.
6. Block out bright ambient light with a sunscreen to maximize the light from the flash.
7. Focus on the bottom of the impression, not on the scale. Take an existing- or reflected-light photograph.
8. Position the flash at a very low angle (10–15 degrees) to the impression. This will enhance the detail of the impression. For consistent exposure, hold the flash at least 5–7 feet from the impression. Shoot several exposures, bracketing toward overexposure to obtain maximum image detail. Move the flash two or more angles to the impression.
9. Take the exposures, move the light to another position, adjust the sunscreen, and repeat Steps 7 and 8.

Impressions in Snow

Impressions in snow are difficult to photograph because of lack of contrast. First, attempt to photograph the impressions as if in soil. To increase the contrast, lightly spray snow impressions with Snow Print Wax, a material used for casting snow impressions, or with colored spray paint. Hold the spray can at least 2–3 feet from the impression so the force of the aerosol does not damage the impression. Direct a light application of spray at an angle of about 30–45 degrees so the colored paint strikes only the high points of the impression. Highlighted impressions will absorb heat from the sun and must be shielded until photographed and cast to prevent melting.

Recovering the Original Evidence

Whenever possible, submit to the Laboratory the evidence bearing the original impression. If the evidence cannot be submitted to the Laboratory, use the following techniques to recover the evidence.

Casting Three-dimensional Impressions

Casting a three-dimensional impression in soil, sand, or snow is necessary to capture detail for examination. Dental stone, with a compressive strength of 8,000 psior greater, must be used for casting all impressions. The compressive strength is listed on the container along with the proper ratio of powder to water used for mixing. Dental stone is available through local dental supply houses. Colored dental stone is preferred.

Plaster of paris, modeling plasters, and dental plasters are not sufficiently hard, do not resist abrasion when cleaned, and must not be used.

Mixing Dental Stone in a Bag

Store dental stone in resealable plastic bags. An 8- by 12-inch resealable plastic bag can store two pounds of dental stone powder. With premeasured bags, casting impressions at the crime scene involves only adding water. The bag containing the dental stone powder can be used to mix and pour the dental stone.

To make a cast, add the appropriate amount of water to the bag and close the top. Mix the casting material by vigorously massaging it through the bag for 3–5 minutes. Ensure that the material in the corners of the bag is also mixed. After it has been mixed, the material should have the consistency of pancake batter or heavy cream.

Mixing Dental Stone in a Bucket or Bowl

If the impressions are numerous or large, it may be necessary to mix larger quantities of dental stone in a bucket or bowl. The dental stone should be added slowly to the water and stirred continuously for 3–5 minutes. After it has been mixed, the material should have the consistency of pancake batter or heavy cream.

Pouring Dental Stone

Casting material has sufficient weight and volume to erode and destroy detail if it is poured directly on top of the impression. The casting material should be poured on the ground next to the impression, allowing it to flow into the impression. The impression should be filled with casting material until it has overflowed.

If the mixture does not flow easily into all areas of the impression, use a finger or a small stick on the surface to cause the dental stone to flow into the impression. Do not put the stick or finger more than 1/4 inch below the surface of the casting material because it can damage the impression.

Before the cast hardens completely, write the date, collector's initials, and other identifying information on it. In warm weather, the cast should be left undisturbed for at least 20–30 minutes. In cold weather, the cast should be left undisturbed longer. Casts have been destroyed or damaged when lifted too soon. If the cast is in sand or loose soil, it should lift easily. Casts in mud or clay may require careful treatment and excavation when being removed.

Allow the cast to air-dry for at least 48 hours. Package the cast in paper, not in plastic. An FBI Laboratory examiner must clean the cast.

Lifting Two-dimensional Impressions

Lifting an impression allows for the transfer of a two-dimensional residue or dust impression to a lifting film. It also allows the impression to be shipped to the Laboratory for photographing and examination.

Electrostatic Lifts

An electrostatic lifting device lifts footwear impressions from porous and non-porous surfaces without damaging the impressions. This device works on dry dust or residue impressions on clean surfaces but will not work if the impressions were wet or have become wet. Electrostatic lifting devices come with instructions for use.

Storing Electrostatic Lifting Film

Lifted impressions are damaged easily if the film is not stored properly. The film has a residual charge that attracts dust and debris and causes the film to cling to other surfaces. To preserve and store the lifting film containing an impression, tape one edge of the film securely in a clean, smooth, high-quality paper file folder or tape the edges securely in a shallow photographic paper box. Low-grade cardboard boxes such as pizza boxes must not be used because the residual charge on the film will pull dust from the box and contaminate the impression.

Items that contain a dry residue footwear impression must not be wrapped or stored in plastic because a partial transfer of the impression to the plastic will occur

Gelatin and Adhesive Lifts

Gelatin lifters can be used to lift impressions from porous and non-porous surfaces. Black gelatin lifters work well for lifting light-colored dry or wet impressions. White gelatin lifters can be used to lift impressions developed with fingerprint powders or impressions dark enough to contrast with a white background.

Adhesive lifters can be used only to lift impressions from smooth, non-porous surfaces. White adhesive lifters can be used to lift impressions developed with fingerprint powders. Transparent adhesive lifters can be used to lift impressions developed with black or fluorescent powders. Transparent tapes such as two-inch fingerprint-lifting tape also can be used to lift powdered impressions if the impressions are transferred to a white card.

Lifting Materials

- *Electrostatic* can be used on porous and non-porous surfaces. Used to lift dry dust and residue impressions. Nondestructive. Useful for searching for latent impressions.
- *White adhesive* can be used on smooth, non-porous surfaces. Used to lift wet or dry impressions that have been chemically enhanced or developed with dark fingerprint powder.
- *Transparent adhesive* can be used on smooth, non-porous surfaces. Used to lift wet or dry impressions that have been treated with black or fluorescent fingerprint powder. Do not use on an original impression.
- *White gelatin* can be used on all porous and non-porous surfaces as long as the gelatin contrasts with an impression. Used to lift wet or dry impressions that have been chemically enhanced or developed with fluorescent fingerprint powder.
- *Black gelatin* can be used on all porous and non-porous surfaces. Used to lift wet or dry impressions. Offers good contact with most residue.

Searching Shoe Print and Tire Tread Files

A file of shoe manufacturers' designs and a file of tire treads and other reference material can be searched to determine brand names and manufacturers.

Questions concerning shoe print and tire tread evidence should be directed to 703-632-7288, 703-632-7314, or 703-632-7315. Follow the evidence submission directions, including **Requesting Evidence Examinations** and **Packaging and Shipping Evidence**.

- For shoe print and tire tread comparisons, submit original evidence whenever possible (shoes, tires, photographic negatives, casts, lifts).
- For shoe print and tire tread file searches, submit quality photographs of the impressions. If photographs are not available, submit casts, lifts, or the original evidence. Detailed sketches or photocopies are acceptable. Images of impression evidence may be submitted electronically. Call **703-632-7288** for specifics on submitting evidence in this manner.
- Unobtrusively write the collector's initials, dates, and other relevant information on the evidence.
- Air-dry and package evidence separately in Bubble Wrap; clean, smooth, high-quality paper or laminated folders; or paper bags, depending on the items being submitted for examination.

Soil Examinations

Soil examinations can determine whether soils share a common origin by comparing color, texture, and composition.

Questions concerning soil evidence should be directed to 703-632-8449. Follow the evidence submission directions, including **Requesting Evidence Examinations** and **Packaging and Shipping Evidence**.

- Collect soil samples as soon as possible, because the soil at the crime scene can change dramatically.
- Collect soil samples from the immediate crime scene area and from the logical access and escape route(s).
- Collect soil samples where there are noticeable changes in color, texture, and composition.
- Collect soil samples at a depth that is consistent with the depth from which the questioned soil may have originated.
- If possible, collect soil samples from alibiareas such as the yard or work area of the suspect(s).
- Submit a map identifying soil-sample locations.
- Do not remove soil adhering to shoes, clothing, and tools. Do not process tools for latent prints. Air-dry the soil and the clothing, and package separately in paper bags.
- Carefully remove soil adhering to vehicles. Air-dry the soil, and package separately in paper bags.
- Ship known and questioned debris separately to avoid contamination. Submit known and questioned soil in leak-proof containers such as film canisters or plastic pill bottles. Do not use paper envelopes or glass containers. Pack to keep lumps intact.

Special-event and Situational Awareness Support

Visual information specialists travel to the field and conduct digital site/venue surveys. These operations include three-dimensional laser scanning and documentation of physical structures and objects, 360-degree spherical video capture, and geographic information system (GIS) mapping.

Questions concerning special-event and situational awareness support should be directed to 703-632-8194.

Tape Examinations

Tape composition, construction, and color can be compared with known sources. Comparisons can be made with the torn end of tape and a suspect roll of tape.

The Laboratory will examine duct, vinyl electrical, packaging, masking, and cellulose acetate (e.g., Scotch) tapes.

Questions concerning tape evidence should be directed to 703-632-8441. Follow the evidence submission directions, including **Requesting Evidence Examinations** and **Packaging and Shipping Evidence**.

- Whenever possible, submit tape still adhered to the substrate. This minimizes the loss of trace evidence, latent fingerprints, or contact impressions. If it is not possible to submit the substrate, the tape may be manually removed and placed adhesive side down on a clean, colorless piece of plastic sheeting (e.g., transparency film or Kapak tubular rollstock), not on cardboard, paper, or vinyl document protectors. Do not distort or tear the tape during removal.
- If the tape is cut during removal, document and initial each cut. Use a method that produces a unique cutting pattern (e.g., pinking shears).

Toolmark Examinations

Tools can bear unique microscopic characteristics because of manufacturing processes and use. These characteristics can be transferred to surfaces that had contact with the tools. Evidence toolmarks can be compared with recovered tools. In the absence of a questioned tool, toolmark examinations can determine the type of tool(s) that produced the toolmark and whether the toolmark is of value for comparison. Toolmark examinations also include lock-and-key examinations.

Fractures

Fracture examinations sometimes can be used to determine whether evidence was joined together and subsequently broken apart.

Questions concerning toolmark evidence should be directed to 703-632-8442. Follow the evidence submission directions, including **Requesting Evidence Examinations** and **Packaging and Shipping Evidence**.

- If possible, submit the tool-marked evidence.
- If it is not possible to submit the tool-marked evidence, make a cast to submit to the Laboratory.

1. Use an acrylic-surface replica cast kit. Call the Laboratory at **703-632-8442** regarding the appropriate cast kit.
2. Different formulas are used in different temperatures. If possible, move the evidence to a warm area.
3. Casts will duplicate foreign material in the stamped characters. Clean the area before proceeding. Remove paint and dirt with a solvent such as acetone, gasoline, or paint remover. Use Naval Jelly to remove rust. Use a soft brush. Do not use a wire brush.
4. Build a dam around the stamped characters to retain the acrylic liquid while it hardens. Use a soft and pliable dam material such as modeling clay. Ensure there are no voids in the dam.
5. Following the instructions in the kit, mix the liquid and powder for one minute and pour the mixture into the dam.

6. The acrylic liquid will take 30 minutes to harden. Remove the cast when it is hard. If paint and rust are on the cast, make additional casts and submit the cleanest one to the Laboratory.
7. Indicate where on the object (often a vehicle) the cast was taken.
8. Pack the cast to prevent breakage.

- Photographs locate toolmarks but are of no value for identification purposes.
- Obtain samples of any material deposited on the tools. Submit samples in leak-proof containers such as film canisters or plastic pill bottles.
- To avoid contamination, do not place the tool against the tool-marked evidence.
- Submit the tool rather than making test cuts or impressions.
- Mark the ends of the evidence and specify which end was cut during evidence collection.

Toxicology Examinations

The Toxicology discipline of the FBI Laboratory is accredited by the American Board of Forensic Toxicologists. Toxicology examinations can disclose the presence of drugs and poisons in biological specimens and food products. The examinations can determine the circumstances surrounding drug- or poison-related homicides, suicides, and accidents.

Because of the large number of potentially toxic substances, it may be necessary to screen for classes of poisons. Examples include:

- Volatile compounds (ethanol, methanol, isopropanol).
- Heavy metals (arsenic).

- Non-volatile organic compounds (drugs of abuse, pharmaceuticals)
- Miscellaneous (strychnine, cyanide).

Questions concerning toxicology evidence should be directed to 703-632-8441. Follow the evidence submission directions, including **Requesting Evidence Examinations** and **Packaging and Shipping Evidence**.

- Accepting evidence in alleged poison investigations will be based on whether the victim(s) sought medical attention or a suspicious death occurred. A doctor's medical evaluation and report must be included with the evidence.
- Biological evidence in drug-facilitated assaults must include a urine sample. The urine must be collected as soon as possible after the assault but must not have been collected more than 96 hours after the alleged drugging.
- Toxicological analysis of hair specimens will be performed only for specific drugs or poisons. **Call the Laboratory at 703-632-8441 prior to submitting hair to ensure that the evidence will be accepted for examination.** The communication accompanying the evidence must reference the telephone conversation accepting the evidence.
- The quantity of biological specimens submitted depends on whether the identity of a toxic substance is known, the route of administration, the time after exposure that biological specimens are collected, and whether subjects(s) or victim(s) are living or deceased. **Call the Laboratory at 703-632-8441 prior to submitting the specimens to ensure that the correct quantity is submitted.** The communication accompanying the evidence must reference the telephone conversation accepting the evidence.

- Each biological specimen must be placed in separate, labeled, sealed glass tubes, plastic cups, or heat-sealed or resealable plastic bags. Affix BIOHAZARD labels to the inside and outside containers.
- Refrigerate or freeze biological specimens during storage and shipping to prevent deterioration. Pack so that no breakage, leakage, or contamination occurs.
- Submit a copy of the autopsy or incident report.
- Describe the symptoms of the suspect(s) or victim(s) at the time of the crime or prior to the death.
- List any known or questioned drugs consumed by or prescribed for the suspect(s) or victim(s).
- Describe any known or questioned environmental exposure to toxic substances by the suspect(s) or victim(s).

Video Examinations

Video examinations are conducted by the FBI's Operational Technology Division (OTD), Digital Evidence Laboratory (DEL), Forensic Audio, Video, and Image Analysis Unit (FAVIAU). The OTD DEL has different acceptance criteria and a different physical address than the FBI Laboratory, as described below.

Authenticity

Authenticity examinations are conducted to determine whether video recordings are original, continuous, unaltered, and consistent with the operation of the recording device used to make the recording.

Enhancement

Enhancement examinations are conducted to maximize the clarity of the video signal.

Video Image Processing

Enhanced still images can be produced from images on video and made as prints or digital files.

Standards Conversion

Video can be converted from one standard to another (e.g., PAL to NTSC or SECAM).

Format Conversion

Video can be converted from one format to another (e.g., Beta to VHS).

Synchronization

Audio and video signals can be combined to produce one composite recording.

Special Effects

Special effects, such as a mosaic or blur spot, can be added to video recordings to protect a person's identity.

Damaged Media Repair

Video recordings can be repaired, restored, or retrieved for playback and examination, if damage is not too extensive.

Questions concerning video examinations should be directed to 703-985-1393. Questions concerning video evidence should be directed to 703-985-1388.

Video examinations may not be submitted directly from entities outside the FBI. State, local, or international agency cases must be submitted by the FBI field office servicing the area and must meet one of the following two criteria: 1) the state, local, or international case has a nexus to an ongoing FBI investigation or 2) the FBI division head deems that the case is of enough regional importance to merit the dedication of federal resources to the state, local, or international case. These criteria shall be met with a written statement from the division head (Special Agent in Charge). FBI entities may submit cases directly.

Follow the evidence submission directions, including **Requesting Evidence Examinations** and **Packaging and Shipping Evidence**.

- Write-protect the original media. Never use the Pause operation when viewing original video recordings.
- Submit original video recordings. If originals cannot be obtained, call for further instructions.
- Queue the original videotape to the approximate time of the pertinent area. State in a communication the date and time of the pertinent area, and use the date-time stamp on the video or the counter indicator (set from the beginning of the tape at 000).
- Label the outer container "FRAGILE, SENSITIVE ELECTRONIC EQUIPMENT" or "FRAGILE, SENSITIVE AUDIO/VIDEO MEDIA" and "KEEP AWAY FROM MAGNETS OR MAGNETIC FIELDS".
- Address the outer container as follows:

Forensic Program, Building - 27958A, Engineering Research Facility, Federal Bureau of Investigation, Quantico - VA 22135

Weapons of Mass Destruction Examinations

A weapon of mass destruction (WMD) is typically associated with nuclear and/or radiological, biological, or chemical agents; however, it also may be an explosive. WMDs are designed to cause a large amount of destruction or disruption to people and infrastructures.

The FBI Laboratory has formalized partnerships with a variety of government, academic, and private laboratories to conduct forensic examinations of evidence that either contains or is contaminated with hazardous chemical, biological, and/or radiological material.

Depending on the nature of the threat—i.e., chemical, biological, or radiological—evidence examinations will be conducted by the Laboratory or at a designated FBI partner laboratory specially equipped to handle hazardous materials.

The Laboratory can direct or apply the use of specialized analytical techniques to identify and characterize a wide range of biological pathogens, toxins, chemical agents, toxic chemicals, and trace radioactive compounds that constitute a suspected or potential WMD.

The FBI's Hazardous Evidence Analysis Team (HEAT), composed of forensic examiners and technicians from the various FBI Laboratory disciplines, is trained to safely conduct traditional examinations of hazardous evidence. These examinations are conducted at FBI partner laboratories.

Suspected or confirmed WMD crime scenes should be handled only by qualified personnel.

Upon notification or suspicion of a possible WMD incident, contact the FBI's Strategic Information and Operations Center at 202-323-3300 and ask for the Weapons of Mass Destruction Operations Unit Duty Officer.

Before it can be analyzed by the Laboratory or partner laboratories, suspected or confirmed WMD evidence must be properly field-screened by qualified personnel to determine the absence or presence of hazardous materials. **Questions concerning WMD evidence examinations should be directed to 703-632-7766.**

Wood Examinations

Wood examinations can match sides, ends, and fractures; determine wood species; and compare wood particles found on clothing, vehicles, and other objects with wood from the crime scene.

Questions concerning wood evidence should be directed to 703-632-8449. Follow the evidence submission directions, including **Requesting Evidence Examinations** and **Packaging and Shipping Evidence**.

- Submit wood in plastic or paper bags.

Chapter 3

Crime Scene Safety

Personnel have the ultimate responsibility to recognize chemical, biological, and physical hazards when processing a crime scene. However, it is the responsibility of each agency responding to and providing support at the crime scene to develop policies, programs, and training on health and safety practices.

Always consult local, state, and federal environmental and occupational health and safety laws when working with forensic evidence. All shipping of forensic evidence must comply with US Department of Transportation and International Air Transport Association regulations.

This section describes the hazards, safety precautions, safe work practices, and personal protective equipment recommended for personnel processing routine crime scenes. This section also explains the importance of complying with waste-disposal regulations.

Routes of Exposure

Personnel operating in or around contaminated environments must be aware of the various ways in which hazards may enter and harm the body.[1]

Inhalation

Inhalation is the introduction of a toxic product by the respiratory system. Airborne contaminants may be in the form of a dust, aerosol, smoke, vapor, gas, or fume. Materials may be in a solid or liquid form and still represent an inhalation hazard because they produce vapors, mists, and fumes.

Proper work practices and adequate ventilation can minimize the risk of airborne-contaminant inhalation. When working in areas with airborne contaminants present, personnel must wear respiratory protection. Personnel must be certified to wear respiratory protection and, therefore, to work in areas containing airborne contaminants.

Skin Contact

Contamination through the skin can result from direct contact or by absorption. The severity of the injury can depend on the concentration of the contaminant and the amount of exposure time. Systemic effects—such as dizziness, tremors, nausea, blurred vision, liver and kidney damage, shock, or collapse—can occur when the substances are absorbed through the skin and circulated throughout the body. Exposure can be prevented by using personal protective equipment (e.g., gloves, safety glasses, goggles, face shields, and protective clothing).

Ingestion

Ingestion involves introducing contaminants into the body through the mouth. Ingestion can cause severe damage to the mouth, throat, and digestive tract. To prevent entry of contaminants into the mouth, safe work practices—such as washing hands before eating, smoking, or applying cosmetics—must always be used. Personnel should not bring food, drinks, or cigarettes into areas where contamination can occur, regardless of personal protection they may be wearing.

Injection

The direct injection of contaminants into the body—either by needle sticks or mechanical injuries from contaminated glass, metal, or other sharp objects—can cause severe complications. Contaminants enter directly into the bloodstream and can spread rapidly. Extreme caution should be exercised when handling objects with sharp or jagged edges. Work gloves must be worn at all times.

Safety

Bloodborne Pathogen Safety

On December 6, 1991, OSHA issued Title 29, Section 1910.1030, of the Code of Federal Regulations (CFR), *Bloodborne Pathogens.*[2]

Occupations at risk for exposure to bloodborne pathogens include law enforcement, emergency response, and forensic laboratory personnel.

Fundamental to the bloodborne pathogens standard is the concept of following universal precautions. This concept is the primary mechanism for infection control. It requires that employees treat all blood, body fluids, or other potentially infectious materials as if infected with bloodborne diseases, such as the hepatitis B virus (HBV), the hepatitis C virus (HCV), and the human immunodeficiency virus (HIV). The following protective measures should be taken to avoid direct contact with potentially infectious materials:

Use barrier protection—such as disposable gloves, coveralls, and shoe covers—if contact with potentially infectious materials may occur. Change gloves when torn or punctured or when their ability to function as a barrier is compromised. Wear appropriate eye and face protection to protect against splashes, sprays, and spatters of potentially infectious materials.

Wash hands after removing gloves or other personal protective equipment. Remove gloves and other personal protective equipment in a manner that will not result in contaminating unprotected skin or clothing.

Prohibit eating, drinking, smoking, or applying cosmetics where human blood, body fluids, or other potentially infectious materials are present, regardless of personal protection that may be worn.

Place contaminated sharps in appropriate closable, leak-proof, puncture-resistant containers when transported or discarded. Label the containers with a BIOHAZARD warning label.

Do not bend, re-cap, remove, or otherwise handle contaminated needles or other sharps.

After use, decontaminate equipment with a daily prepared solution of household bleach diluted 1:10 or with 70 per cent isopropyl alcohol or other appropriate disinfectant. Non-corrosive disinfectants are commercially available. It is important to allow sufficient contact time for complete disinfection.

In addition to universal precautions, engineering controls and prudent work practices can reduce or eliminate exposure to potentially infectious materials. Examples of engineering controls include long-handled mirrors used to locate and retrieve evidence in confined or hidden spaces and puncture-resistant containers used to store and dispose of sharps and paint stirrers.

Chemical Safety

Depending on the type of material encountered, a variety of health and safety hazards can exist. Some of these hazards are identified by the following categories:[13]

- Flammable or combustible materials—such as gasoline, acetone, and ether—ignite easily when exposed to air and an ignition source, such as a spark or flame.
- Over time, some explosive materials, such as nitroglycerine and nitroglycerine-based dynamite,

deteriorate to become chemically unstable. In particular, ether will form peroxides around the mouth of the vessel in which it is stored. All explosive materials are sensitive to heat, shock, and friction.

- Oxidizers—such as nitrates, hydrogen peroxide, and concentrated sulfuric acid—are chemical compounds that readily yield oxygen to promote combustion. Avoid storage with flammable and combustible materials or substances that could rapidly accelerate their decomposition.
- Corrosive materials can cause destruction to living tissue or objects such as wood and steel. The amount of damage depends on the concentration and duration of contact.
- When working with chemicals, be aware of hazardous properties, disposal techniques, personal protection, packaging and shipping procedures, and emergency preparedness. This awareness comes from appropriate training and the information in a Material Safety Data Sheet. The Material Safety Data Sheet provides information on the hazards of a particular material so that personnel can work safely and responsibly with hazardous materials.

Light-source Safety

When using ultra-violet lights, lasers, and other light sources, personnel must protect their eyes from direct and indirect exposure.[4] Not all laser beams are visible, and irreversible eye damage can result from exposure to direct or indirect light from reflected beams. Prolonged exposure to the skin also should be avoided.

All personnel in the vicinity of the light source should wear protective eyewear appropriate for the light source. Goggles must have sufficient protective material and fit snugly to prevent light from entering at any angle. The goggles must display the American National Standards Institute's (ANSI's) mark denoting eye-protection compliance. Laser-protective eyewear must be of the appropriate optical density to protect against the maximum operating wavelength of the laser source.

Confined-space Safety

A confined space is an enclosed area large enough for personnel to enter and work, but it has limited or restricted means for entry and exit. Confined spaces (e.g., sewers, open pits, tank cars, and vats) are not designed for continuous occupancy. Confined spaces can expose personnel to hazards including toxic gases, explosive or oxygen-deficient atmospheres, electrical dangers, or materials that can engulf personnel entering the space.[5]

Conditions in a confined-space must be considered dangerous, and personnel may not enter the space until a confined-space permit has been issued. The atmosphere must be monitored continuously with a calibrated, direct-reading instrument for oxygen, carbon monoxide, flammable gases and vapors, and toxic air contaminants. Periodic readings from these monitors should be documented. Only certified confined-space personnel may operate in confined-spaces. Rescue services must be immediately available to the site.

The following practices must be followed when working in a confined space:

- Never enter before all atmospheric, engulfment, mechanical, and electrical hazards have been identified and documented. Isolating hazards must be performed in accordance with OSHA 29 CFR 1910.147, *The Control of Hazardous Energy (Lockout/Tagout)*.[6]
- Provide ventilation. Ensure that ventilation equipment does not interfere with entry, exit, or rescue procedures.

- Provide barriers to warn unauthorized personnel and to keep entrants safe from external hazards.
- Provide constant communication between personnel entering the confined space and attendants.
- Ensure that back-up communication is in place prior to entry.
- Wear appropriate personal protective equipment, such as self-contained breathing apparatus (SCBA), a full-body harness, head protection, and other necessary equipment.
- Never attempt a rescue unless part of a designated rescue team.
- Ensure that personnel certified in first aid and CPR (cardiopulmonary resuscitation) are on-site.
- For additional information, refer to the OSHA standard for *Permit-Required Confined Spaces*, 29 CFR 1910.146.[7]

Excavation Safety

All excavations must meet the requirements set forth in OSHA's standards for excavations, 29 CFR 1926.650,[8] 1926.651,[9] and 1926.652.[10] Each employee in an excavation shall be protected from cave-ins by an adequate protective system designed in accordance with 29 CFR 1926.652(b) or 29 CFR 1926.652(c),[10] unless excavations are less than five feet in depth and examination of the ground is made by a competent person to prevent cave-ins. A competent person is someone capable of identifying existing and predictable hazards in the surroundings or working conditions that are unsanitary, hazardous, or dangerous to employees and who has the authorization to take prompt corrective action to eliminate those hazards.

As with all excavations, personnel should be aware of buried utilities and control standing water, hazardous environments, confined spaces, and oxygen-deficient atmospheres.

X-Ray Safety

Portable, handheld X-ray machines, often used to identify the contents of unknown packages, pose a risk for exposure to X-ray radiation at crime scenes.

Keep X-ray exposure as low as reasonably achievable by adhering to the following:

- Shield the X-ray device, the questionable object, and the operator.
- Remove all non-essential personnel from the X-ray field.
- Limit the time that personnel must be in the area of operation.
- Always wear assigned monitoring devices appropriate for X-ray radiation.
- Ensure that standard X-ray operating procedures are in place and followed and that adequate training has been provided in accordance with federal and state regulations.

Personal Protective Equipment

At all crime scenes, the selection of personal protective equipment must be done in coordination with a hazard risk assessment completed by trained and qualified personnel. The hazard risk assessment should identify the possible contaminants as well as the hazards associated with each product. Depending on the outcome of the assessment or uncertainty of the hazards associated with the given scene, OSHA's standard for *Hazardous Waste Operations and Emergency Response*, 29 CFR 1910.120,[11] may need to be applied. Entry into these types of scenes will depend on each law enforcement organization's available equipment, situational training, and qualified personnel.

Hand Protection

Hand protection should be selected on the basis of the type of material being handled and the hazard(s) associated with the material.[12, 13] Detailed information can be obtained from the manufacturer. The following list provides information about glove material types and functions:

- Nitrile provides protection from acids, alkaline solutions, hydraulic fluid, photographic solutions, fuels, lubricants, aromatics, petroleum, and chlorinated solvents. It also offers some resistance to cuts and snags.
- Neoprene offers resistance to oil, grease, acids, solvents, alkalies, bases, and most refrigerants.
- Poly-vinyl chloride (PVC) is resistant to alkalies, oils, and limited concentrations of nitric and chromic acids.
- Latex (natural rubber) resists mild acids, caustics, detergents, germicides, and ketonic solutions. Latex will swell and degrade if exposed to gasoline or kerosene. When exposed to prolonged, excessive heat or direct sunlight, latex gloves can degrade, causing the glove material to lose its integrity.
- Using powder-free gloves with reduced protein content reduces the risk of developing latex allergies. Personnel allergic to latex usually can wear nitrile or neoprene.

Guidelines for glove use include the following:

- Prior to donning gloves, inspect them for holes, punctures, and tears. Remove rings or other sharp objects that can cause punctures.

- When working with heavily contaminated materials, wear a double layer of gloves.
- Change gloves when they become torn or punctured or when their ability to function as a barrier is compromised.
- To avoid contaminating unprotected skin or clothing, remove disposable gloves by grasping the cuffs and pulling them off inside out. Discard disposable gloves in designated containers. Do not reuse.

Eye Protection

Personnel handling chemical, biological, and radioactive materials should wear appropriate eye protection, such as safety glasses and goggles.[1, 14] Face shields offer better protection when there is a potential for splashing or flying debris. Face shields must be worn in combination with safety glasses or goggles because face shields alone are not considered appropriate eye protection.

Contact lens users must wear safety glasses or goggles to protect the eyes. In the event of a chemical splash into the eye, it can be difficult to remove the contact lens to irrigate the eye, and contaminants can be trapped behind the contact lens.

Protective eyewear also should be worn over prescription glasses. Alternately, safety glasses may be made to the wearer's eyeglass prescription.

Foot Protection

Shoes that completely cover and protect the foot are essential.[12, 15] Protective footwear should be worn at crime scenes when there is a danger of foot injuries from falling or rolling objects, from objects piercing the sole, or from exposure to electrical hazards. The standard recognized by OSHA for protective footwear is the *American National*

Standard for Personal Protection—Protective Footwear, ANSI Z41-1991.[16] In some situations, non-permeable shoe covers can provide barrier protection to shoes and prevent the transfer of contamination outside the crime scene.

Respiratory Protection

Certain crime scenes, such as bombings and clandestine laboratories, can produce noxious fumes and other airborne contaminants in which responders must use respiratory protection.[1, 12, 17]

Compliance with 29 CFR 1910.134, *Respiratory Protection*, 18 is mandatory whenever respirators are used. Critical elements for the safe use of respirators include a written program, training, medical evaluation, fit testing, and a respirator maintenance program. Without these elements, the wearer is not guaranteed protection.

Head Protection

At certain crime scenes where structural damage has occurred or may occur, protective helmets should be worn. The standard recognized by OSHA for protective helmets is ANSI's requirements for industrial head protection, Z89.1-2003.[19]

Hazardous Materials Transportation

All shipments of suspected or confirmed hazardous materials must comply with US Department of Transportation and International Air Transport Association regulations. Title 49 of the CFR lists specific requirements that must be observed when preparing hazardous materials for shipment by air, land, or sea.[20] In addition, the International Air Transport Association annually publishes *Dangerous Goods Regulations*,[21] which details how to prepare and package shipments for air transportation.

Title 49 CFR 172.101 provides a Hazardous Materials Table22 that identifies items considered hazardous for the purpose of transportation. Title 49 CFR 172.101 also addresses special provisions for certain materials, hazardous materials communications, emergency response information, and training requirements for shippers. Personnel who serve any function in the shipment of hazardous materials must receive the specified training prior to shipping any materials by commercial transportation.

Hazardous Waste Regulations

The US Environmental Protection Agency's Resource Conservation and Recovery Act (RCRA),[23] commonly referred to as the "cradle-to-grave" regulation, was established to track chemicals from "cradle," or generation, to "grave," or disposal. This system imposes requirements on both generators and transporters, as well as on transport, storage, and disposal facilities. RCRA specifies that once a material is determined to be hazardous, it becomes the generator's complete responsibility.

The process for determining whether a material is a hazardous waste should be completed by qualified personnel. Even new material in its original container may be considered waste if there is no use for it. The services of a hazardous waste contractor and transporter can be used to help remove materials from scenes. Hazardous materials that are removed from crime scenes are considered evidence and would not fall under RCRA waste provisions. However, when a case has been adjudicated or, for other reasons, the material is not needed, the immediate assistance of a qualified contractor knowledgeable about local regulations must be sought. Clandestine drug laboratories and environmental crime scenes are examples of situations that may require the removal of waste.

References

1. National Research Council. Committee on Hazardous Substances in the Laboratory. *Prudent Practices for Handling Hazardous Chemicals in Laboratories*. National Academy Press, Washington, DC, 1981.

2. *Bloodborne Pathogens*, 29 CFR 1910.1030, US Department of Labor, Occupational Safety and Health Administration, Washington, DC Available: http://www.osha.gov/pls/oshaweb owadisp.show_document?p_table=standards&p_id=10051.

3. Upfal, MJ *Pocket Guide to First Aid for Chemical Injuries*. Genium, Schenectady, New York, 1993.

4. American National Standards Institute. *American National Standard for Safe Use of Lasers* (ANSI Z136.1-2000). American National Standards Institute, New York, 2000.

5. Conforti, JV *Confined Space Pocket Guide*. Genium, Schenectady, New York, 1996.

6. *The Control of Hazardous Energy (Lockout/Tagout)*, 29 CFR 1910.147, US Department of Labor, Occupational Safety and Health Administration, Washington, DC Available: http://www.osha.go pls/oshaweb owadisp.show_document?p_table=standards&p_id=9804.

7. *Permit-Required Confined Spaces*, 29 CFR 1910.146, US Department of Labor, Occupational Safety and Health Administration, Washington, DC Available: http://www.osha.gov/pls/oshaweb/ wadisp.show_document?p_table=standards&p_id=9797.

8. *Scope, Application, and Definitions Applicable to This Subpart*, 29 CFR 1926.650, US Department of Labor, Occupational Safety and Health Administration, Washington, DC Available:http://www.osha.gov/ plsoshawebowadisp.show_document?p_table= standards&p_id=10774.

9. *Specific Excavation Requirements*, 29 CFR 1926.651, US Department of Labor, Occupational Safety and Health Administration, Washington, DC Available: http://www.osha.gov/pls/oshaweb/owadisp.show_document?p_table=standards&p_id=10775.

10. *Requirements for Protective Systems*, 29 CFR 1926.652, US Department of Labor, Occupational Safety and Health Administration, Washington, DC Available: http://www.osha.gov/pls/oshaweb/owadisp.show_document?p_table=standards&p_id=10776.

11. *Hazardous Waste Operations and Emergency Response*, 29 CFR 1910.120, US Department of Labor, Occupational Safety and Health Administration, Washington, DC Available: http://www.osha.gov/pls/oshaweb/owadisp.show_document?p_table=standards&p_id=9765.

12. Office of Environmental Health and Safety. *Laboratory Survival Manual*. University of Virginia, Charlottesville, Virginia, 1998. Available: http://ehs.virginia.edu/chem/home.html.

13. Choose the proper gloves for chemical handling. In: *Best's Safety Directory*. AM Best, Oldwick, New Jersey, 1998.

14. American National Standards Institute. *American National Standard Practice for Occupational and Educational Eye and Face Protection* (ANSI Z87.1-2003). American National Standards Institute, New York, 2003.

15. *Occupational Foot Protection*, 29 CFR 1910.136, US Department of Labor, Occupational Safety and Health Administration, Washington, DC Available: http://www.osha.gov/pls/oshaweb/owadisp.show_document?p_table=standards&p_id=9786.

16. American National Standards Institute. *American National Standard for Personal Protection—Protective Footwear* (ANSI Z41-1991). American National Standards Institute, New York, 1991.

17. Gorman, C. *Hazardous Waste Handling Pocket Guide.* Genium, Schenectady, New York, 1997.

18. *Respiratory Protection,* 29 CFR 1910.134, US Department of Labor, Occupational Safety and Health Administration, Washington, DC Available: http://www.osha.gov/pls/oshaweb/owadisp.show_document?p_table=standards&p_id=12716.

19. American National Standards Institute. *American National Standard for Personnel Protection—Protective Headwear for Industrial Workers—Requirements* (ANSI Z89.1-2003). American National Standards Institute, New York, 2003.

20. *Transportation,* 49 CFR 100–185, US Department of Transportation, Washington, DC Available: http://www.access.gpo.gov/nara/cfr/waisidx_05/49cfr172_05.html.

21. International Air Transport Association. *Dangerous Goods Regulations.* 44th ed., Montreal, Canada, 2003.

22. Hazardous Materials Table, 49 CFR 172.101, US Department of Transportation, Washington, DC Available: http://www.access.gpo.gov/nara/cfr/waisidx_05/49cfr172_05.html.

23. *Resource Conservation and Recovery Act,* 40 CFR 3001–3020, US Environmental Protection Agency, Washington, DC Available: http://www.epa.gov/region5/defs/html/rcra.htm.

Chapter 4

Crime Scene Search

Crime scenes involving suspected or confirmed weapons of mass destruction (WMD) (nuclear and/or radiological, biological, chemical, or explosive agents) should be handled only by qualified personnel. The FBI is the lead federal agency of a suspected or confirmed WMD crime scene. Specific information on how to process a hazardous materials crime scene is not covered in this section. Upon notification or suspicion of a possible WMD incident, contact the FBI's Strategic Information and Operations Center at 202-323-3300 and ask for the Weapons of Mass Destruction Operations Unit Duty Officer.

A crime scene search is planned, coordinated, and executed by law enforcement officials to locate physical evidence.

Basic Principles

- The best search options are usually the most difficult and time-consuming.
- Physical evidence cannot be over-documented.
- There are two search approaches:
  1. A cautious search of visible areas, avoiding evidence loss or contamination.

2. A vigorous search of concealed areas.

Preparation

- Obtain a search warrant, if necessary.
- Discuss the search with involved personnel before arriving at the scene, if possible.
- Establish a command headquarters for communication and decision-making in major or complicated crime scene searches.
- Ensure that personnel are aware of the types of evidence usually encountered and the proper handling of the evidence.
- Make preliminary personnel assignments before arriving at the scene, if possible.
- Establish communication between the medical examiner, laboratory personnel, and prosecutive attorneys so that questions that arise during the crime scene search can be resolved.
- Coordinate agreements with all agencies in multi-jurisdictional crime scene searches.
- Accumulate evidence collection and packaging materials and equipment.
- Prepare the paperwork to document the search.
- Provide protective clothing, communication, lighting, shelter, transportation, equipment, food, water, restroom facilities, medical assistance, and security for search personnel.
- In prolonged searches, use shifts of two or more teams. Transfer paperwork and responsibility in a preplanned manner from one team to the next.
- Ensure that assignments are in keeping with the attitude, aptitude, training, and experience of search

personnel. Personnel may be assigned two or more responsibilities:

Team Leader

- Ensure scene security.
- Prepare administrative log.
- Conduct preliminary survey (initial walk-through).
- Prepare narrative description.
- Resolve problems.
- Make final decisions.

Photographer

- Photograph and log evidence and scene.

Sketch Preparer

- Sketch and log scene.

Evidence Recorder

- Serve as evidence custodian and log evidence.

Evidence Recovery Personnel

- Ensure that evidence is located and documented (photo and sketch). Initial and date all evidence collected.

Specialists

Brought in from the FBI Laboratory, private industry, academia, other laboratories, etc., on a case-by-case basis to assist in their area of expertise.

Should be identified prior to the time they are actually needed.

Approach

- Be alert for evidence, especially transient evidence.

- Take extensive notes.
- Consider the safety of all personnel.

Secure and Protect

- Take control of the scene immediately.
- Determine the extent to which the scene has been protected. Obtain information from personnel who have knowledge of the original condition.
- Continue to take extensive notes.
- Keep out unauthorized personnel.
- Record who enters and leaves.

Preliminary Survey

The preliminary survey is an organizational stage to plan for the search.

- Cautiously walk through the scene.
- Maintain administrative and emotional control.
- Select a narrative technique (written, audio, or video).
- Take preliminary photographs.
- Delineate the extent of the search area. Expand the initial perimeter as needed.
- Organize methods and procedures.
- Recognize special problem areas.
- Identify and protect transient physical evidence.
- Determine personnel and equipment needs. Make specific assignments.
- Determine the need for any specialists.
- Develop a general theory of the crime.

- Take extensive notes to document the scene, physical and environmental conditions, and personnel movements.

Evaluate Physical Evidence Possibilities

This evaluation begins upon arriving at the scene and becomes detailed in the preliminary survey stage.

- Ensure that collection and packaging materials and equipment are sufficient.
- Focus first on evidence that could be lost. Leave the least transient evidence for last.
- Consider all categories of evidence possibilities.
- Search the easily accessible areas and progress to out-of-view locations. Look for hidden items.
- Evaluate whether evidence appears to have been moved inadvertently.
- Evaluate whether the scene appears contrived.

Narrative

The narrative is a running description of the crime scene.

- Use a systematic approach in the narrative.
- Nothing is insignificant to record if it catches one's attention.
- Under most circumstances, do not collect evidence during the narrative.
- Use photographs and sketches to supplement, not substitute for, the narrative.
- The narrative should include the following:
    - Case identifier.

  - Date, time, and location.
  - Weather and lighting conditions.
  - Identity and assignments of personnel.
  - Condition and position of evidence when an evidence recovery log is not used.

Photography

- Photograph the crime scene as soon as possible.
- Prepare a photographic log that records all photographs and a description and location of evidence.
- Establish a progression of overall, medium, and close-up views of the crime scene.
- Photograph from eye level to represent the normal view.
- Photograph the most fragile areas of the crime scene first.
- Photograph all evidence in place prior to recovery.
- All items of evidence should be photographed by close-ups, first without a scale and then with a scale, filling the frame.
- Photograph the interior crime scene in an overlapping series using a normal lens, if possible. Overall photographs may be taken using a wide-angle lens.
- Photograph the exterior crime scene, establishing the location of the scene with a series of overall photographs including a landmark. Photographs should have 360 degrees of coverage. Consider using aerial photography, when possible.
- Photograph entrances and exits from the inside and the outside.
- Prior to entering the scene, acquire—if possible—prior photographs, blueprints, or maps of the scene.

Sketch

The sketch establishes a permanent record of items, conditions, and distance and size relationships.

- Sketches should supplement photographs.
- Sketch number designations should coordinate with the evidence log number designations.
- The sketch should include the following:
  - Case identifier.
  - Date, time, and location.
  - Weather and lighting conditions.
  - Identity and assignments of personnel.
  - Dimensions of rooms, furniture, doors, and windows.
  - Distances between objects, persons, bodies, entrances, and exits.
  - Measurements showing the location of evidence. Each object should be located by at least two measurements using an established measurement system, e.g., triangulation, transecting baseline, or azimuth.
  - Key, legend, compass orientation, scale, scale disclaimer, or a combination of these features.

Conduct Detailed Search

- Use a search pattern (grid, strip or lane, or spiral).
- Search for evidence from the general to the specific.
- Be alert for all evidence.
- Search entrances and exits.

Record and Collect Physical Evidence

- Ensure that all items are photographed prior to collection.
- Mark evidence locations on the sketch.
- Complete an evidence log noting all items of evidence collected. If possible, have one person serve as evidence custodian.
- Two people should observe the evidence in place, then as it is collected, initialed, and dated. Evidence items are marked directly only when positive the marks will not interfere with subsequent forensic examination.
- Wear latex or cotton gloves to avoid leaving fingerprints.
- Do not excessively handle the evidence after recovery.
- Seal all evidence packages at the crime scene.
- Obtain known standards (e.g., fiber samples from a known carpet).
- Constantly check paperwork, packaging, and other information for errors.

Final Survey

- The final survey is a review of all aspects of the search.
- Discuss the search with all personnel.
- Ensure that all documentation is correct and complete.
- Photograph the scene showing the final condition.
- Ensure that all evidence is accounted for before departing the scene.

- Ensure that all supplies and equipment are removed from the scene.
- Ensure that no areas have been overlooked in the detailed search.
- Reconsider the need for additional specialists.

Release

- Release the crime scene after the final survey.
- The scene should be released only when all personnel are satisfied that the scene was searched correctly and completely.
- Only the person in charge should release the scene.
- Ensure that the appropriate inventory has been provided, consistent with legal requirements, to the person to whom the scene is released.
- Crime scene release documentation should include the time and date of release, to whom released, and by whom released.
- Once the scene has been released, reentry may require a warrant.

Index

Other Bestselling Books

Intelligence Tradecraft: Secrets of Spy Warfare, by MK Dhar (former Joint Director, IB)

Manas Police & Security Yearbook 2010-2011 (fully Illustrated) by Ajit Doval IPS, BR Lall, IPS and other Top Cops.

Manas Defence Year Book 2010-2011 (Fully Illustrated) by General S Padmanabhan and Lt Gen S Pattabhiraman

CBI Top-Cop Recalls by SK Dutta, IPS (Former Director – CBI)

Pakistan's Intelligence by Sudhakar Raje (Ex-Indian Diplomat)

Who Runs Police: Secrets of a Top Cop by HS Swan, IPS (Ex-DGP, Haryana)

Why Police Fails: Confessions of a Top Cop by Vinay Kumar Singh, IPS

Police and Naxalism: Strategies for Solutions by ML Kumawat, IPS, Nazrul Islam, IPS and others

Common Man's Guide to Police & Criminal Laws by Dr DV Guruprasad, IPS (DG – Karnataka Police)

Rainbow People: Reinventing Northeast India by Falguni Rajkumar, IAS (Former Sec NEC)

Industrial Security: Management & Strategies by DC Nath, IPS & Capt SB Tyagi

Naxalism: Causes and Cure by PK Agrawal, IAS

Financial Terrorism: Black Money and the Indian Elite by BR Lall, IPS (Former: Joint Director, CBI)

Intelligence for Management by DC Pathak, IPS (Former Dir-Intelligence Bureau)

Effective Interrogation: Naxalism, Police, Intelligence by G Chatterjee (Former Intelligence Officer)

White Collar Crimes X-Posed by Thakur Shailendra Nath

Intelligence, Security & Asymmetric Warfare by Dhirendra Singh, IAS and Lt Gen DB Shekatkar

Inside IB and RAW: The Rolling Stone that Gathered Moss by K Sankaran Nair, IPS (Former Head: Research and Analysis Wing (RAW)

Intelligence: Corporate Success and Vigilance by D C Pathak, IPS (Ex Chief – IB)

The Undisclosed Punjab: India Besieged by Terror by Birbal Nath, IPS (Former DGP, Punjab)

The Folds of Insurgency by AP Maheshwari, IPS

Who Owns CBI: The Naked Truth by BR Lall, IPS (Former: Joint Director, CBI)

Saga of Civil Services by Dr Yogendra Narain, IAS (Former Defence Secretary)

Open Secrets: India's Intelligence Unveiled by M K Dhar, IPS

Security Manual by P Benjamin

SPYMASTER: My Life in the CIA by Ted Shackley

VIP Security: What You Need to know by Kanchan Sinha

Armed Forces Tribunal by Dr UC Jha

Jungle Warfare: An Ultimate Handbook by Dr NC Asthana, IPS

Ultimate Handbook of Urban Warfare by Dr NC Asthana, IPS

Beyond North East: Insurgency-History-Development by HN Das (Former Chief Secretary, Assam)

Why Bureaucracy Fails by Kalyan Ray, IAS

WMD Terrorism: Strategy for Consequences Management

by Brig MS Patial

Intelligence Manual by Department of Defence, USA

The ISI Game Plan by Brig Yash Mohan, VSM

Terror, Insurgency and the State: Ending Protracted Conflicts by Marianne Heiberg etc.

Operation Triple X: An Indian Spy-Run in Pakistan A Novel by MK Dhar, IPS

Legal Safeguards for Defence Personnel by Air Cmde. Ranvir Kumar (Former Judge Advocate General)

Reforming Intelligence Agencies: Pakistan's Transitional Democracy by Frederic Grare

Combating Terrorism: Strategies of Ten Countries by Yonah Alexander

Strategies in Defence and Intelligence by Lt Gen S Pattabhiraman & MK Dhar, IPS

Sports, Games and Adventure Sports by Air Cmde (Dr) CN Ghosh

The Craft of Intelligence by Allen W Dulles

Fulcrum of Evil: ISI-CIA-Al Qaeda Nexus by MK Dhar (Former Joint Chief of IB)

The Conspirators: Fiction of Facts (A Book on Pakistan's Intelligence) by Brig Yash Mohan, VSM

Silent Warfare: Understanding the World of Intelligence

by Abram N Shulsky & Gary J Schmitt

Wages of Crime: Black Markets, Illegal Finance and the Underworld Economy by R T Naylor

The Peace Keepers: Indian Police Service (IPS) by SR Arun, IPS

Para-Military Forces: Central Reserve and Foreign Policy

by Dr AK Pasha

Human Rights Training by Dr S Subramanian, IPS

Industrial Espionage: Causes and Cure by Dr S Subramaniam, IPS

Executive Protection by Dr S Subramaniam, IPS

CIA's Eye on South Asia by Anuj Dhar, Journalist

Threat to Security: How Secured is India from within by PC Dogra, IPS (Former DGP, Punjab)